Badminton

Jack Reznik
Ron Byrd
Louisiana State University

Gorsuch Scarisbrick, Publishers
Scottsdale, Arizona

Consulting Editor for the Lifetime Sport and Fitness Series: Robert P. Pangra...
Chairman of the Department of Physical Education • Arizona State Univers...

Editor: *Wayne Schotanus*
Production Manager: *Gay Orr*
Manuscript Editor: *Charlene Brown*
Cover Design: *Gordon Fong, The Omni Group*
Photographs: *Jon Fisher*
Typesetting: *Carlisle Graphics*
Layout: *Bill Nebel, Graphic Arts Services*
Printing and Binding: *BookCrafters*

Gorsuch Scarisbrick, Publishers
8233 Via Paseo del Norte, Suite E-400
Scottsdale, Arizona 85258

10 9 8 7 6 5 4 3 2 1

ISBN 0-89787-604-0

Printed in the United States of America.

Preface

The fitness boom is in high gear, and more and more people are participating in some form of sports activity. We now realize that regular participation in a vigorous sports activity, such as badminton, can improve both our physical appearance and our physical condition. The purpose of this book is to help you learn and improve your badminton skills. As you improve your skills, you will find yourself playing badminton regularly, enjoying hours of fun and improving your physical conditioning at the same time.

This book has systematic and easy to follow instructions to assist you in developing the various skills associated with successful badminton play. It progresses from introductory skills to advanced skills. It offers guidelines for the selection of equipment, detailed explanations of strokes and serves, and discussions of singles, doubles, and mixed doubles strategies. All instructions are accompanied by photographs and illustrations to help you visualize and accomplish the various strategies, strokes, and serves.

A detailed section of assignments and drills is provided to help you practice and perfect your skills. This unique feature allows you to develop the skills in logical progression, and skills tests are provided so that you can measure your progress at regular intervals. Logs to record your test results are provided in the appendixes at the back of the book.

Finally, this book discusses methods for improving your muscular and cardiorespiratory fitness for successful badminton play and better overall fitness. We have included information about weight control, goal setting, and warm-up and cool-down exercises. We hope that this detailed guide will improve your badminton game significantly and encourage you to play regularly. See you on the court!

Jack Reznik
Ron Byrd

Contents

1
The Game of Badminton

The game of badminton can be played either indoors or out-of-doors. As a competitive sport, however, the game is usually played indoors on an artificially lighted court. Two players (singles) or four players (doubles) may participate.

Object of the Game

The main objective in badminton is to hit the shuttlecock, more commonly called the *bird,* over the net with a racquet in such a way that one's opponent will not be able to successfully return it. This can be accomplished by using any of a variety of shots, ranging from the spectacular smash to the delicate drop.

Origin of the Game

Two thousand years ago, children of early China played with an object that resembled a shuttlecock. A similar game was played in Europe over a thousand years later, but the modern game originated in India, where it remains an important national sport. English colonists learned to appreciate the game, named it *badminton,* and spread it with their empire around the world. Today, England, Denmark, and Canada have outstanding players, but the best are found in Southeast Asia (Malaysia and Indonesia), Japan, and China, where the game is almost a way of life.

General Rules of Play

In men's singles and all doubles competition, play continues until a player or team scores 15 points. In women's singles, the first player to score 11 points wins. However, if the score is tied at 13–all or 14–all in 15-point contests (9–all or 10–all in 11-point games), then the player or team to first reach the tied score may *set* the game. (See Scoring below.)

Play is initiated with an underhand stroke (serve) from the right-hand service court diagonally to the player standing in the opposite right-hand service court. Once a legal service is completed, the bird is *in play.* The receiver must return the bird before it touches the floor.

With only one hit, the player must send the bird over the net to the opponent's court. The bird continues to be struck alternately by opposing players until it touches the floor, is hit illegally, gets stuck in the net, or some other fault occurs.

If the receiver or receiving side fails to make a legal return, a point is awarded to the serving side. Only the serving side can score points. When the serving side fails to return the bird successfully, a loss of serve occurs.

The play between serves is called a rally. During a rally, the bird can only be touched once before it must travel over the net to the opponent's side of the court. In doubles, both partners may swing at the bird, but only one can hit it.

Before you play a game or match, learn the rules. A thorough understanding of them will allow you to concentrate on the other rudiments of play (i.e., positioning, stroking, and strategy). Study the outline of rules adapted from the American Badminton Association in Chapter 3.

Singles

In singles, one player plays against another. Singles is more demanding physically than doubles because one player has to cover an entire court on his or her side of the net. Consequently, a player (1) needs to be in good condition to play at full speed throughout a match, (2) must have quick reflexes and effective anticipation in order to get a good *jump* on the bird, and (3) must have *fast feet* to cover the court, retrieve the bird, and return to a good base position.

In singles, the server's score determines from which side of the court the bird will be served. If the server's score is 0 or an even number, the serve must be delivered from the right-hand service court. When the server's score is an odd number, then the serve is initiated from the left-hand service court. The server must move to the alternate court to initiate the next serve. This procedure of alternating serves continues as long as the server wins points.

Doubles

Doubles consists of two teams with two players on each side. This method of play is less physically demanding than singles because the task of covering the court is divided between the two partners. Shots must be placed more accurately and aggressively to win a rally since more players are available to cover the court. A good doubles team is a cohesive unit of two players who work well together. Such a team can make greater use of planning strategy. (See Doubles Strategy in Chapter 8.)

Scoring and serving in doubles are similar to scoring and serving in singles, with a few variations. The team that is serving is called the *in side,* and the receiving team the *out side.* At the beginning of each game, only one player on the serving side serves. The first service during each inning begins from the right-hand service court and must be hit diagonally to the opposing, right-hand service court. If the rally is won, the same serving player initiates play from the left-hand service court, and so on. When the serving team loses a rally in the first inning, the serve then passes to the opposing team. From this time, both players from each side have the opportunity to serve before service passes to the opposing team. In other words, the serving team may lose two rallies before losing service.

The area of the court that you or your partner must occupy when serving or receiving the serve is determined by your side's score. For example, at the start of play, if you begin the serve from the right-hand service court, you will always begin or receive the serve from this court area when your side's score is zero or an even number. Likewise, your partner will initiate or receive the serve from the right-hand service court when your team's score is an odd number. After the shuttle is in play, you or your partner may maneuver anywhere on the court. The rally continues with each team hitting the bird alternately over the net. Either partner may return the bird when it is in play.

Scoring

Initially, keeping track of the score may present a problem to the novice player. Once you play several games, however, scoring will become quite easy to do. A regulation game consists of 15 points for men's singles and all doubles play, 11 points for women's singles.

Only the serving side can score points. As long as your side scores points, you or your partner continues to serve. A side must win two of three games to win the match.

If the score is tied at 1 or 2 points less than the amount needed to complete regulation play, the player or team that reaches the tied score first has the option of increasing the number of points necessary to win the game or letting it end in regulation play. The term used to increase the score is called *setting*.

When the score is tied at 13–13 for games consisting of 15 points, the player or team first reaching it may set the game to 5 more points or let it end at 15 points. For games tied at 14–all and not previously set, one has the option of increasing the final score needed to win the game by 3 points. In women's singles, the game may be set to 3 points when the score is tied at 9–all and to 2 points when tied at 10–all.

The choice of setting the score and the number of points needed to win must be made immediately after the score is tied and prior to the next service. This amounts to increasing the score either to 18 (or 17 points) for games normally ending at 15 points or to 12 points for those ending at 11 points.

Whenever a game is set, players customarily call the score *love–all*. Then the new score begins.

Benefits of Play

The reasons for playing badminton are many and varied. The court is relatively small, rules are easy to learn, equipment and space requirements are minimal, enjoyment can be derived from playing, carryover value for other sports is great, and injuries are rare. Badminton also offers many physiological, psychological, and sociological benefits to those who participate on a regular basis. Another advantage is that persons of all sizes can play successfully, taller players not having the advantage in badminton that they do in most other team sports.

Improved physical fitness is one of the major benefits of regular play. If you play at least three times per week for one or more hours per session, you can improve your cardiorespiratory endurance significantly. In addition, you can strengthen several areas of your body such as your wrists, arms, and legs. Playing badminton can also improve your flexibility and neuromuscular coordination. Badminton is an efficient way to exercise. This activity consumes a lot of energy in a short period of time, making it an ideal method of working out for people on tight schedules. The length of the rallies between skilled, evenly matched opponents requires a heavy expenditure of calories.

Although the rallies in badminton are longer than in most racquet sports, you can vary the intensity of play by the type of shot you execute. You can end a rally quickly with a smash, or you can prolong it with clears. By playing doubles instead of singles, you can lessen the intensity of the workout because you have a smaller area of the court to cover and you do not have to run as much.

Many players experience psychological benefits from regular play. One of the primary ones is the release of tension and stress. Vigorous physical activity can give you a chance to relax mentally, to get away, and to forget for a while the pressures and tensions brought about by your job and society. These psychological releases result from the intense concentration needed to watch and hit the bird as well as to implement complex strategies of play. In order to be successful, you must give the game your undivided attention. You have no time to think about anything other than what shot to hit next. Besides emotional release, you can also experience intense mental satisfaction. This exhilarating feeling can result from making a super shot, watching your opponent run to retrieve a difficult return only to have it fall short, or engaging in an exceptional rally. This wonderful feeling can also come from upsetting a better or more experienced opponent. At the conclusion of a match, just knowing that you exercised vigorously contributes to this feeling of well-being. In other words, your psychological need to play, to have fun, and to express your emotions may be partially met by participating in this sport. Badminton can be an excellent means of helping you to maintain good mental health. Sociologically, it can provide an avenue to meet and interact with people of all ages and from different walks of life. It can afford the opportunity to communicate with people regardless of their sex, social position, or ethnic background and to widen your circle of friends. Badminton is also an excellent game for family participation and enjoyment.

As previously mentioned, the risk of injury is slight. With the exception of a few minor aches and pains generally associated with engaging in a strenuous physical activity, rarely does a badminton player experience injury. The ultralightweight equipment precludes even tennis elbow or tendonitis.

The skills and techniques used in badminton can be effectively carried over into other activities. They can be utilized in such sports as racquetball, tennis, paddleball, and squash.

All of these values make badminton a fascinating and stimulating sport for persons of all ages. Once learned, this activity can serve as an enjoyable hobby and a way of maintaining physical and emotional health in our fast-paced world.

Badminton Governing Agencies

The American Badminton Association is affiliated with the worldwide governing agency, the International Badminton Federation. Both function to promote the sport, to organize and sanction tournaments, and to set rules of play. These organizations publish journals that sell for nominal prices and contain a wide variety of articles and reports. Information regarding subscriptions and memberships can be obtained from the American Badminton Association, 1330 Alexandria Drive, San Diego, CA 92107.

Etiquette and Courtesies of Play

Badminton is a more enjoyable game to play when certain amenities are observed throughout a contest or match. The way you act in a given situation often makes the difference between a pleasant or an unpleasant experience. Courteous behavior is always dictated.

Most games are played informally without the services of a referee. Unless all players observe the rules and courtesies associated with play, these contests can deteriorate into something other than badminton. All the participants should know and understand the rules; however, it is equally important that all players exhibit acceptable social behavior. The latter point may be defined as the employment of good sportsmanship, which includes how you conduct yourself and the courtesy you extend to others throughout the entire match.

During play, unsportsmanlike conduct should neither be displayed nor tolerated. Always try your best to win by utilizing your own skills within the rules of play—not to win at any cost. Following are social amenities that should be adhered to in both formal and informal play:

- Show up on time for a scheduled match.
- Introduce yourself to your opponents, the referee, and others present prior to play.
- Warm up with your opponents until everyone is ready to play.
- Call "ready" before serving.
- Announce the score prior to serving (server's score first).
- Return the shuttle to the server as quickly as possible following the rally.
- Accept and abide by all the decisions of the referee.
- Replay all questionable calls.
- Accept your opponent's decision.
- Call all decisions on your side of the court immediately and fairly.
- Call all of your own carries, throws, slings, out-of-bounds, or other faults.
- Control your emotions.
- Keep conversation to a minimum during play.
- Compliment your opponent or your partner after the rally ends when a good shot has been made.
- Retrieve the shuttle from another court only after the rally in that court has ended.
- Never walk behind the baseline or across a court during a rally.
- Play doubles instead of singles when other players are waiting to play.
- Congratulate your opponents after the match when they have won, or thank them for playing.

2
Badminton Terminology

To properly appreciate the game and to be able to "speak the language" of badminton, even beginners should become familiar with and routinely use the following terms:

Ace: A winning service that eludes a receiver.

Alley: The extension of the width of the singles court on both sides by 1½ feet for doubles play.

Back Alley: The area between the baseline and the long service line for doubles.

Backcourt: See Back Alley.

Backhand: The stroke hit from the side opposite the forehand.

Backswing: The initial swing of the racquet in a backward direction in preparation for hitting the shuttle.

Balk: A deceptive movement made with the intent of deceiving an opponent prior to or during the service. Also called a *feint.*

Base: The strategic area of the court to which a player should move after playing a shot. It is located in the center of the court about two feet behind the short service line.

Baseline: The back boundary or farthest line from the net at either end of the court.

Bird: Officially called the *shuttlecock* but commonly referred to as the *shuttle.* It is the missile hit back and forth over the net during play.

Block: The act of placing one's racquet in front of the oncoming shuttle, causing the shuttle to rebound into the opponent's court. No swing is involved. The racquet strings do all the work.

Carry: An illegal shot in which the shuttle momentarily rests on the racquet and is slung or hit twice before going over the net.

Center: See Base.

Clear: A high, deep shot hit near the baseline of the court.

Combination formation: A method of doubles play that incorporates all the other systems of doubles play. *See also* I Formation, Side-by-Side Formation, and Up-and-Back Formation.

Court: The area of play for badminton.

Crosscourt shot: Any shot hit diagonally from one side of the court to the opposite side.

Deception: The act of deceiving an opponent by changing at the last second the speed and the direction of the shuttle. *See also* Balk.

Defense: The side receiving the serve. Or, the side that is kept on the run, out of position, or unable to make a placement to open the court to their advantage.

Double hit: The act of hitting the shuttle twice in succession on the same stroke. Sometimes called a *carry.*

Doubles: Competitive or match play between two teams of two players on each side.

Doubles service court: The area within the centerline, the outer side boundary line, and the short and rear service lines.

Down-the-line: A shot hit parallel and close to the sideline.

Drive: A shot that sends the shuttle in a low and flat trajectory over the net at a high rate of speed.

Drive clear: A type of shot that passes with a relatively flat trajectory over an opponent's head.

Drive serve: A serve that is hit hard with a relatively flat trajectory.

Drop shot: A deftly controlled finesse or soft shot designed to barely clear the net with minimum force.

End: One half or side of the badminton court.

Face: The stringed hitting surface of the racquet.

Fault: A violation of the rules of play. This term is mainly used in conjunction with violations of serving and receiving rules.

First serve: A term in doubles play used to denote that the person serving is the first server of the side.

Flat: When the flight of the shuttle is a level, horizontal trajectory.

Flick: A shot made to speed up the shuttle with a quick movement of the wrist and little or no arm motion. It is generally used to change the pace of a shot hit below net level and to send the shuttle high and deep to the backcourt, catching one's opponent off guard.

Follow-through: A continuation of the swing after the shuttle has been contacted that contributes to the shot's control and direction.

Foot fault: Illegal positioning or moving of the feet while serving.

Forecourt: The area of the court between the net and the front service line.

Forehand: The stroke used to hit the shuttle on the racquet side of a player, palm forward.

Frontcourt: *See* Forecourt.

Front service line: The line 6½ feet from and parallel to the net on each side of the court that forms the forward boundary of the service court.

Game: Competition concluded when one player or team scores 15 points (or 11 points for women's singles). *See also* Setting.

Game bird: The point that decides the winner of the game.

Grips: Various ways of holding the racquet.

Hairpin: A shot made from very close to and below the net, with the flight of the shuttle traveling up and barely clearing the net before it descends close to the net on the other side.

Half-court shot: A low shot hit to the midcourt of the opponent. It is mainly used in doubles play, especially against the **I** Formation.

Head: The part of the racquet that includes the frame and the strings.

High serve: A serve that is hit high and deep into the receiver's court.

IBF: International Badminton Federation. Founded in 1934, it is the sport's world governing body.

I Formation: See Up-and-Back Formation.

Inning: A round of play in which a player or team holds service.

In play: The period of time during which the shuttle is legally rallied, beginning with the serve and ending when the shuttle touches the floor or a fault or a let occurs.

In side: The player or team serving.

Kill: A fast, downward shot that is either impossible or almost impossible to return. *See also* Putaway and Winner.

Let: A legitimate stoppage of play that allows the exchange or rally to be replayed.

Lob: See Clear.

Lob serve: See High Serve.

Long serve: A serve that lands beyond the baseline in singles play or beyond the long service line in doubles.

Long service line: The back service line in doubles play beyond which the shuttle may not be served.

Loose shot: A weakly hit shot.

Love: The term used to denote no score.

Love–All: This means that both players or teams have no score and are tied at 0 to 0. The term is also used when a game has been set. *See also* Setting.

Low serve: A softly hit serve that barely skims over the net.

Match: A contest concluded when a player or team wins two of three games.

Match point: The point which, if scored, determines the winner of the match.

Midcourt: The area on each side of the court halfway between the net and the baseline.

Mixed doubles: A doubles game in which a male and a female play as partners on each side.

Net: The piece of equipment that divides the court into two equal parts and over which the shuttle must be hit.

Net play: Action that takes place near the net.

Net shot: A shot played from the forecourt near the net.

Nonracquet arm: The arm opposite to the arm that holds the racquet.

Nonracquet foot: The foot opposite to the side of the body where the racquet is held.

No shot: A call made by players immediately after an illegal shot has occurred.

NYBC: New York Badminton Club. Founded in 1878, this club claims to be the oldest badminton club in the world.

Obstruction: Any interference to an opponent making a shot.

Offense: The attacking side.

Out: When the shuttle touches an area outside the boundary lines of the proper court section.

Out side: The receiving side.

Overhead: A shot hit from a point above the head.

Pass shot: A shot going to either side and beyond the reach of an opponent who is at or approaching the net.

Placement: A shot hit accurately to a predetermined court location where an opponent cannot reach or return it.

Poach: To cut off at the net a shuttle that was intended for your partner.

Point: The unit of scoring earned only by the server or serving team each time the receiver fails to make a legal return.

Push shot: A soft shot made by merely pushing the racquet at the shuttle with little force.

Putaway: See Kill and Winner.

Racquet arm: The arm that holds or normally holds the racquet.

Racquet foot: The foot on the same side of the body as the racquet arm.

Rally: A prolonged exchange of shots after the serve and before point or loss of serve.

Ready position: The body position a player assumes while waiting to receive the serve or return a shot.

Receiver: The player receiving the serve.

Retrieve: To make a good return of a difficult shot to reach.

Return: The hitting back of an opponent's shot.

Round-the-head: An overhead stroke in which the shuttle is contacted above the shoulder of the nonracquet arm. This shot is peculiar to badminton.

Rush the serve: A quick movement to the net in an attempt to put away a low serve by smashing the shuttle down into the opponent's court.

Second service: This indicates that one player of the doubles team has already served.

Serve (service): The act of putting the shuttle into play.

Server: The player who puts the shuttle into play.

Service court: The area on each side of the net bounded by the service, side, base, and center-court lines and into which the serve must be delivered.

Service line: The front line of each service court.

Setting: The method of extending tied games by increasing the number of points necessary to win. The player or team that reaches the tied score first has the option of setting the score.

Setup: A weak return that results in an easy opportunity to hit a shot for a winner.

Shaft: The part of the racquet from the head to the handle.

Short: When a serve causes the shuttle to touch the floor before reaching the proper service court.

Short service line: See Front Service Line.

Shuttle (Shuttlecock): See Bird.

Side-by-side formation: A system of doubles play in which the court coverage and responsibilities are assigned by dividing the court in half.

Sidelines: The lines marking the right and left sides of the court.

Singles: Competition played between two players.

Sling (Throw): See Carry.

Smash: An overhead stroke hit in a downward motion with great speed and power.

Stroke: The act of hitting the shuttle with the racquet.

Switch: When players on a team change court coverage from one side of the court to the other.

Throat: The part of the racquet where the shaft meets the head.

Time-out: A stoppage of play called by either the players or an official.

Up-and-back-formation: A system of doubles play in which a team lines up one in front of the other with the forward player responsible for covering the frontcourt and the other player covering the backcourt.

USBA: United States Badminton Association. The sport's national governing body in the United States.

Winner: A shot that ends a rally. *See also* Kill and Putaway.

Wood shot: The act of hitting the shuttle with the racquet frame.

3
The Laws of Badminton

The laws, or rules, regulating badminton play are set by the International Badminton Federation. These comprehensive laws are occasionally modified, but the basics have changed little over many years. While a complete set of rules may be obtained from the United States Badminton Association, those parts that are most important for beginning and intermediate players have been abstracted here:

- **The Court**
  See Chapter 4, Figure 4.1, for details of the badminton court's dimensions and markings. In brief, the singles court area is 17 feet wide and 44 feet long, and the doubles court is 20 feet wide and 44 feet long. Net height is 5 feet at center and 5 feet, 1 inch, at the posts.

- **The Shuttle**
  Weight of the shuttle should not be lighter than 73 nor heavier than 85 grains. A player with average strength, executing an underhand stroke from the back boundary, should be able to hit the shuttle within 1 to 2½ feet short of the other back boundary.

- **The Players**
  Singles play involves two players—one on each side of the net.

  Doubles competition involves four players—two players per side.

  The side with the serve is called the *in side,* and the receiving side is called the *out side.*

- **The Toss**
  The option of choosing whether to serve first or which court to occupy is assigned by spinning a racquet or tossing a coin. If the winner selects the service option, the loser is entitled to choose on which court he or she wishes to begin play.

- **Scoring**
  Only the server or the server's team can score.

  Doubles and men's singles games are played to 15 points. Women's singles games are decided at 11 points. When a score is tied within 1 or 2 points of the winning score, the first player or team to reach that total has the option of playing to 11 or 15 as originally planned, or of *setting* the game to a certain number of points.

- **The Match**

  The first player or team to win two of three games wins the match. Players or teams change ends (1) after the first game, (2) after the second game, and (3) during the third game (at 8 points in a 15-point game, and at 6 points in an 11-point game). If players forget to change at the regular time, they change as soon as they notice the error. The score remains unaffected.

Table 3.1   Setting Options

Original game	If tied at	May choose to set at
11	9	3 points
11	10	2 points
15	13	5 points
15	14	3 points

- **In Doubles Play**

  At the outset, only one player of the side that starts play is allowed to serve. Subsequently, both players of each team serve during each inning.

  The first serve by a team is from the right-hand service court diagonally to the opponent's right court.

  As long as a team continues to win rallies, the same server continues to serve alternately from the right and left courts, always diagonally to the opponent.

  When the initial server of a team finally loses a rally, the serve passes to the other teammate, who begins serving on the side not used for the preceding service.

  When the score is an even number, players should be on the side where they started. If the score is odd, then their positions should be opposite to the initial arrangement.

  After the serve, both teammates have the right to play any position and to return any shot. The only time that certain players are designated to play the shuttle is on the service. The server is dictated by rule, and only the opponent in the proper receiving court opposite can make the return.

- **In Singles Play**

  Service and return are from the right-hand courts when the server's score is zero or an even number. Conversely, if the player's score is an odd number, service and return must be from the left court.

- **During the Serve**

  If the server misses the shuttle, no fault occurs. The server continues to serve until his or her racquet contacts the shuttle.

  Unlike a server in tennis, the server in badminton is allowed only one contact with the shuttle.

  If a shuttle touches the net on the serve, the bird is considered in play; the decision as to whether the serve is good or bad depends on whether it lands in or out of the defensive service court.

The serve must be underhand, and contact with the bird must be made below the waist. The server's racquet hand must be clearly and discernibly above the entire head of the racquet.

It is a fault for the server's partner in doubles to stand in such a position that the receiver cannot see the shuttle during all parts of the service.

The server's feet must be stationary during the serve. Both the server and the receiver must stand with both feet inside the proper court, not touching the lines.

Neither the server nor the receiver is allowed to make any fakes, feints, or other action designed to gain an unfair advantage during the service.

Neither the server nor the receiver is allowed to delay action unduly in order to gain an unfair advantage. The server may not serve until the receiver is ready. If the receiver tries to return the service, the player is then judged to have been ready. If the receiver is not ready, the receiving player should allow the shuttle to fall uncontested; a let results, and the point is replayed.

The proper service court to which a shuttle should be served is the one diagonally across from the server. A serve that lands outside the boundaries of the proper service court is judged to be out; or shot that lands on the line is considered good.

- **During Play**

A *let* results when a player serves (or in doubles, receives) out of order or from the wrong court. The point is replayed if the player at fault wins the rally and if the mistake is noted before the next serve.

If any serves intervene before the error is noticed, points accrued up to the time of notice and correction stand.

If the player or team at fault loses the rally, a let does not result; the mistake stands uncorrected, and play continues without a change of position.

In the course of match play, the winning player or team serves first in the next game. In doubles, if desired for strategic or other purposes, a different team member may serve first in subsequent games.

As in the serve, a shuttle that lands on a boundary line during the rally is considered to be in the court.

A let is called when anything unusual happens that might interfere with the game, and the point is replayed.

The shuttle may not be struck twice in succession by the same team or player. It may not be held momentarily during a stroke (carry or sling).

Players are not allowed to simply put up their racquets when near the net on the chance that a shuttle return might hit their racquet and rebound over the net. However, players are allowed, even encouraged, to hold their racquets in front of their faces for protection when playing close to the net.

A receiving player may not strike the shuttle before it crosses the net. A player is allowed to follow through across the net but must not strike the net until the shuttle has either hit an opponent or the floor. Play stops immediately upon such contact.

A shuttle is out of bounds if it touches the ceiling, walls, or obstructions. Local rules may be set for arenas with low ceilings or with hanging obstructions.

If the shuttle touches an individual or an individual's clothing, a fault is called against the receiving player, not against the person who made the shot.

Play is continuous, except for five-minute rest periods allowed between games two and three of a match in the United States. Delaying play to recover from fatigue or obtaining advice during a match are grounds for disqualification.

- **Lets and Faults**

In the event of a let, the service is repeated, with no penalty to server or receiver.

Violations in this summary of the rules that are not clearly stated to be lets are termed *faults*. In such cases, the player or team making the error, or faulting, is penalized by losing the point or the serve.

Any serious badminton player should obtain a full set of official rules available from the United States Badminton Association, P.O. Box 237, Swartz Creek, MI 48473.

4
Facilities and Equipment

One of the advantages of badminton as a sport is the minimal equipment and space necessary to play. All you need is a space of approximately 50 feet by 25 feet for the court, a net, a pair of gym shoes, a racquet, and a shuttle, and you are in business!

The Court

The standard badminton court for singles play is 44 feet long and 17 feet wide. It is divided in the middle by a firmly stretched mesh net that is 5 feet high at the center and 5 feet 1 inch high at the posts located on the side boundaries of the court. For doubles play, the width of the court is increased by 3 feet (1½ feet on each side), making the court dimensions 44 feet by 20 feet. The total service area is approximately the same for both singles and doubles play. However, the service court is wider and shorter for doubles (10 feet by 13 feet) as opposed to narrower and longer for singles (8½ feet by 15½ feet). Study the boundaries and service courts diagrammed in Figure 4.1.

Equipment

The equipment needed for play is minimal and can be relatively inexpensive. Most items can be found and purchased in department, discount, and sporting goods stores. Casual attire is acceptable for informal play. However, the sale of sports equipment and clothing is a big business, and the sale of badminton equipment is no exception. Cost and quality can vary significantly. In order to become a more selective consumer, you should familiarize yourself with the wide variety of equipment and clothing available. If possible, seek the advice of a physical education teacher or an experienced badminton player.

Following are some guidelines to assist you in the selection and purchase of equipment and clothing. These guidelines are designed to provide only a starting point of reference, not a prescription. Keep in mind that what works for one player might not work for you. Experiment. Try various racquets, clothing, and shoes until you find what is best for you.

Clothing

Simplicity is the key characteristic of the clothing worn by badminton players. For informal play, men usually wear a short-sleeved shirt or T-shirt and shorts and women wear either a tennis dress or a blouse and shorts or skirt combination. Actually, almost anything goes for in-

Figure 4.1   The badminton court: (A) Singles and (B) doubles.

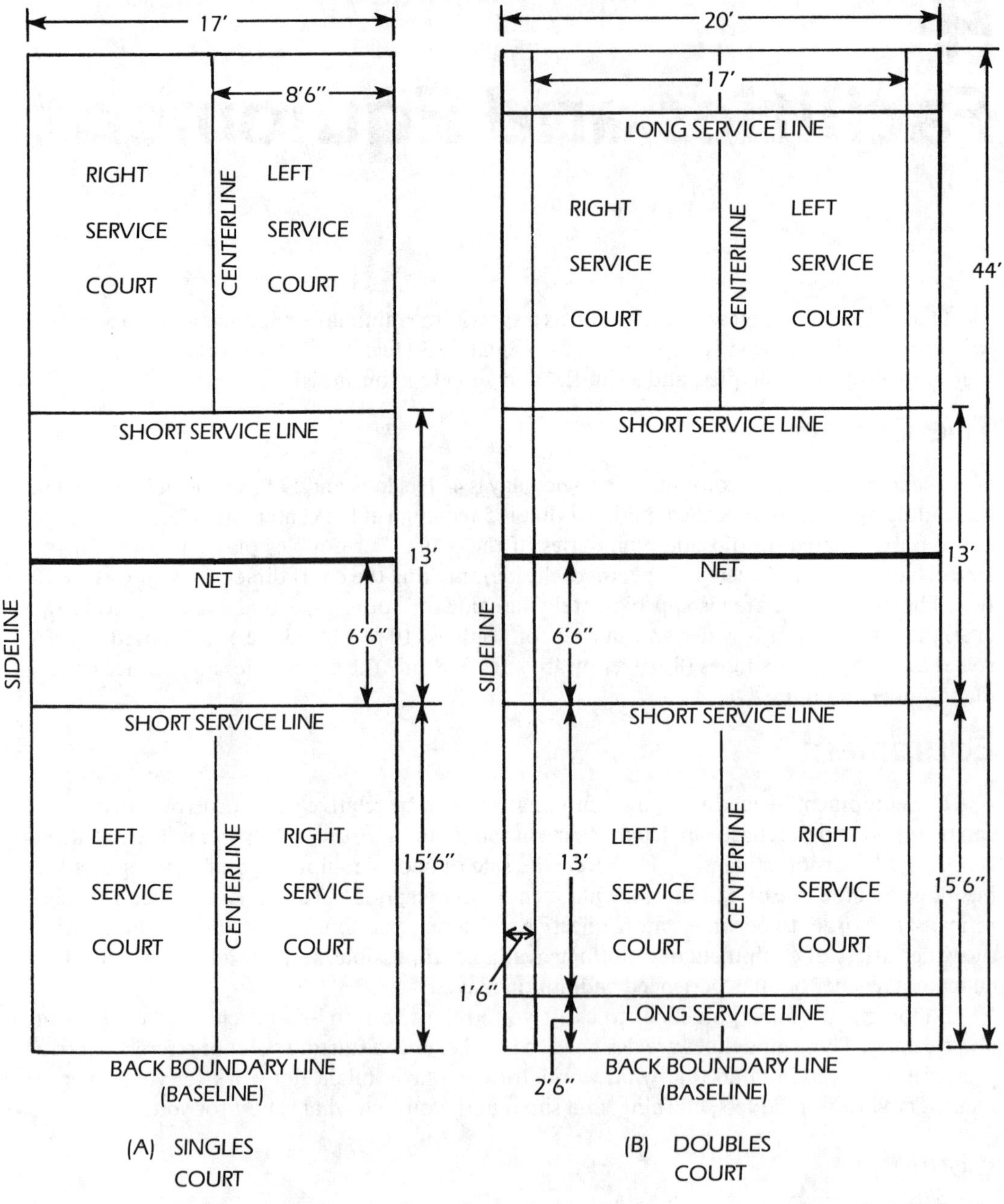

(A)   SINGLES
      COURT

(B)   DOUBLES
      COURT

formal play. The emphasis is on practicality. Clothes should be neither too tight nor too loose. They should allow for freedom of movement. Tight clothing restricts movement, and baggy clothing can hamper your performance. The material should be highly absorbent yet breathable to wick away perspiration and keep you cool during play. Proper attire can prevent excess perspiration from falling to the floor and creating a slippery playing surface.

For formal or tournament play, the traditionally acceptable color for clothing is white. The same guidelines used to select informal clothing are employed in selecting formal attire. (See Figure 4.2.)

Footwear

Choosing the correct shoes for play is very important. Wearing proper-fitting and good-quality shoes will enhance both your comfort and enjoyment of play by providing greater shock absorbency, helping to prevent blisters, giving adequate ankle support, and ensuring good traction. The latter point is especially significant because badminton is a game of quick stops and starts. The ability to maneuver easily on the court is essential. A rough or rippled sole will provide better traction than a smooth one. Either low-cut or high-topped gym shoes may be worn. Although low-cut shoes are preferred by many players, high-topped shoes provide better ankle support.

For added protection for your feet, wear a pair of thick socks. If you have tender feet, wear two pair. This can help to prevent blisters and can supplement the shock absorbency of your shoes. The material should be such that it absorbs perspiration and keeps your feet dry. Your socks should fit snugly but not so tight that they restrict circulation. On the other hand, a loose fitting pair can bunch up or rub and cause blisters. Finally, you should wear a pair of clean socks every time you play. This will help to reduce the breeding ground for bacteria, provide a healthier environment for your feet, and possibly make your shoes wear better and last longer.

Racquets

When purchasing a racquet, buy the best you can afford. The old adage "You get what you pay for" holds true in the badminton racquet market. Selecting a good one is essential be-

Figure 4.2 Clothing. Almost any type can be worn for informal play. The emphasis is on practicality.

cause a poor quality or wrong type of racquet (e.g., wrong weight, improper balance, or wrong grip size) can adversely affect your performance. The racquet is the only link between you and the shuttle. The better its quality and fit, the stronger the connection.

Choosing a racquet is a very personal matter. Before you purchase one, try several different models. If possible, consult a physical education teacher or an experienced player.

Size.   The rules of badminton do not dictate any specifications pertaining to racquet size. However, over the years racquets have evolved to an accepted average length of twenty-six inches. Most racquet heads are oval with the dimensions ten inches by eight inches.

Weight.   Racquets are lighter than they used to be. The average weight of a modern racquet is five ounces or less. Some racquets weigh less than four ounces.

Frame.   The racquet frame is usually all metal or a combination of a metal shaft and a wooden head. Metal racquets are constructed of aluminum or steel. They are more popular and more durable than wooden racquets. Although metal racquets are more expensive, they do not warp and will tolerate more abuse than racquets made from wood. To prevent warping, store a wooden racquet in a racquet press and keep it in a cool place on a flat surface. When strings are broken, they must be repaired immediately or removed entirely until the racquet can be restrung. In selecting a wooden racquet, pay careful attention to the number of laminations. This is an important factor in determining quality—the higher the number of laminations, the stronger the frame. Regardless of what type of frame you select—metal or wood—remember that your racquet is a delicate piece of equipment and treat it as such. With proper care, it will last longer and give you better service.

Handle.   The type of material selected for the handle is a matter of personal preference. Most players prefer the leather grip because it conforms better to the hand. The circumference of the handle varies from 3 ¼ inches to 3 ⅝ inches. Choose one that you can hold comfortably and manipulate easily. Swing the racquet several times to see if it feels heavy or if your fingers feel strained. Racquets that cannot be gripped properly produce finger strain and hand fatigue, which reduces the effectiveness of your strokes. To check the proper handle size, hold the racquet with a forehand grip. Your thumb should wrap around the handle and rest on the first knuckle of your middle finger (see Figure 4.3). If the grip is too large, your thumb will not reach or will barely touch your middle finger. If it is too small, your thumb will extend over the knuckle.

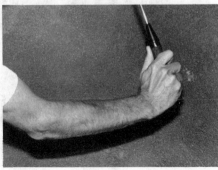

Figure 4.3 Wrist cock (backhand). Extend wrist on backhand side as shown.

Strings.   Racquets are strung with nylon or gut. The level of play determines the type of string utilized. Gut is more expensive and more resilient than nylon. It is preferred by most tournament players because they say they can feel the shuttle on the racquet. However, gut is not practical for most players. It is not moistureproof, and dampness tends to increase tension on the string, often swelling it to the breaking point. For the majority of players, a racquet strung tightly with a good quality nylon is sufficient. Nylon is less expensive than gut, more durable, and provides good service. Keep in mind, as the price decreases, so does the quality of the string.

Generally, strings are purchased according to thickness. The higher the gauge, the thinner the string and the more power that can be added to the shot. The degree of tension is determined both by personal preference and by the manufacturers suggested range for the particular racquet to be strung. In general, racquets are strung at about ten to fourteen pounds of pressure. Tightly strung or higher tension racquets tend to provide more power, but shots are more difficult to control. Do not sacrifice control for added power. The end result will be inconsistent play.

Shuttlecocks

The shuttlecocks, sometimes referred to as shuttles, birds, or birdies, are of two kinds—feathered and synthetic. The latter are usually made of nylon or plastic. They are more durable and less expensive than the feathered shuttles, which top-flight players prefer. The "touch" or "feel" of the shuttle on the racquet and the predictability of its flight are the advantages prized in feathered shuttlecocks. (See Figure 4.4.)

A wide variety of shuttles are available on the market today. Both feathered and synthetic shuttles come in different weights and speeds. The selection of a faster or slower shuttle should be based primarily on environmental conditions. At higher altitudes or in hot playing arenas, the use of slow shuttles is recommended. Conversely, if you are playing in a cold gymnasium, a fast shuttle will make for a better game. When purchasing shuttles, don't try to scrimp. Remember, you get what you pay for in terms of enjoyment, consistency of flight, and development of your ability.

Figure 4.4 Equipment. Select a good racquet; the wrong type can adversely affect your performance. The shuttlecocks are of two kinds, feathered and synthetic.

5
Hitting the Shuttle

To experience success in badminton, one must thoroughly learn and understand sound fundamentals and techniques of play. The degree to which you master these techniques will determine the effectiveness of your game. Practice them until they become second nature to you, and they will greatly enhance your chances of winning and playing well.

The Grips

Holding the racquet correctly is the key ingredient to effective stroke performance. A proper grip is the foundation around which the entire stroke is constructed. An incorrect grip, on the other hand, can lead to inconsistent shot performance. Constantly check and recheck the way you grip your racquet. Remember, the grip affects every shot and provides for a smooth transfer of power from your body to the racquet and eventually to the shuttle.

Forehand Grip

The *shake hands method* is the most common grip used to hold the racquet for the execution of forehand shots. This grip is similar to the forehand grips in other racquet sports such as tennis, racquetball, paddleball, and squash. It is a very natural way to hold the racquet and allows you to both impart power and apply *touch* to shots as needed. (See Figure 5.1.)

To hold the racquet in this manner, place the racquet frame on edge with the short strings perpendicular to the court. Then grasp the handle as if you were shaking hands with a friend. Your palm should be in the same plane as the face of the racquet and lie directly behind the large, flat part of the handle. The fingers should be spread comfortably with the index finger spread slightly away from the other three fingers. The thumb is wrapped around the handle and rests between the first and second fingers of the hand (Figure 5.2). This causes a *V* to be formed by the thumb and index finger on the top of the racquet handle. (See Figure 5.3.)

The racquet should be held firmly, but with an emphasis on feel rather than strength. If you grip the racquet too tightly you will decrease the suppleness of the wrist. There should be no feeling of tension in the wrist. The thumb and index finger provide racquet control and direction. The racquet should be held more with the fingers rather than with the entire hand as in other racquet sports. The handle should rest diagonally across the fingers when using this

Figure 5.1 Forehand grip. With the short strings perpendicular to the court, grasp the handle as if you were shaking hands.

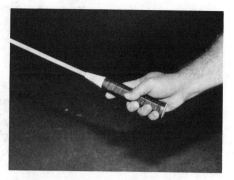

Figure 5.2 Forehand grip (side view). The fingers are spread comfortably, and the thumb is wrapped around the handle and rests between the first and second fingers.

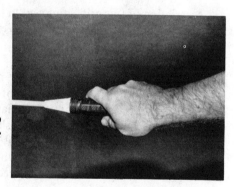

Figure 5.3 Forehand grip (top view). A *V* is formed by the thumb and index fingers.

technique, allowing for the flexibility at the wrist that is required to hit powerful smashes and deceptive drops as well as the maneuverability to change grips from the forehand to the backhand and vice versa.

Backhand Grip

Although you can make shots on the backhand side using a forehand grip, changing your grip slightly to play them is easier. To achieve this grip, hold the racquet with a forehand grip and then turn your hand about an eighth or a quarter turn to the left (to the right, if you are left-handed). Your thumb and index finger should form a *V* on the top, inner bevel of the racquet. The large knuckle of your index finger should lie directly on top of the handle when the racquet face is perpendicular to the floor. Your fingers should be spread comfortably and wrapped around the handle. The thumb rests on the flat side of the handle opposite the first joint of your index finger. This position gives the necessary support needed to hit deep clears and add speed to your drives. (See Figures 5.4 and 5.5.)

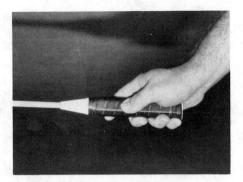

Figure 5.4 Backhand grip (side view). The thumb rests on the flat side of the handle, opposite the first joint of your index finger.

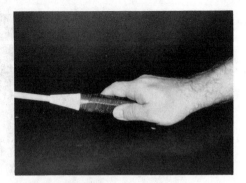

Figure 5.5 Backhand grip (top view). A *V* is formed on the top, inner bevel of the racquet by your thumb and index finger.

A variation of this grip employed to hit backhand shots is to place the thumb on the top, inner bevel of the handle. The index finger and the thumb should be opposite to each other on the handle.

Frying Pan Grip

This grip is only for downward shots such as taps and pushes from near the net. It is a doubles shot, only for use by the *up* player. To assume this grip, simply rotate the racquet ninety degrees from the forehand, handshake grip position. The racquet will be parallel to the floor rather than perpendicular to it as is the case with the forehand grip. As you face the net and raise the racquet, the racquet face will be parallel to the net. This facilitates control, while sacrificing power, and eliminates the need to go from forehand to backhand while defending at the net. (See Figure 5.6.)

Wrist Action

The action of the wrist is an essential element that governs the art of deception in badminton. By wrist action alone, a player can impart speed to the racquet head and produce a powerful snap. To illustrate this point, try hitting the bird without cocking the wrist. You will find that the bird will not travel fast or far. Thus, the choice between executing a smash or a drop shot can be made at the last moment by changing wrist action.

To place your wrist in the proper position (i.e., to cock your wrist) when executing a forehand stroke, grasp the racquet with a forehand grip and take it back to the top of the backswing on the forehand side of your body. At this point, extend your wrist. In the overhand swing, the racquet should be pointing downward, and in the sidearm swing, it should be pointing toward the sideline opposite the one you are facing. (See Figure 5.7.) To achieve the proper wrist cock for the backhand, follow the same general procedure as for the forehand, except on the backhand side. (See Figure 5.8.) Vary the degree you cock your wrist to vary the amount of

Figure 5.6 Frying pan grip. Only for downward shots near the net. Rotate the racquet ninety degrees from the forehand, handshake position.

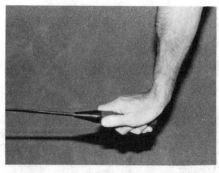

Figure 5.7 Wrist cock (forehand). Extend your wrist as shown.

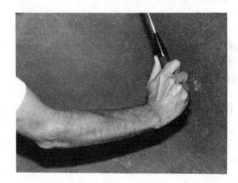

Figure 5.8 Wrist cock (backhand). Extend wrist on backhand side as shown.

power you wish to put into your shot. Remember, you should cock your wrist for all shots for deception purposes and because a certain amount of power is necessary to execute even the most delicate drop shot.

The Ready Position

As you will soon learn, the shuttle crosses the net at various speeds, angles, and heights. Since it rarely crosses the net in the same place, you must be ever alert and prepared to move instantaneously in any direction.

The *ready position* is the stance you should assume while awaiting a serve or return during play. (See Figure 5.9.) This position facilitates quick movements and allows you to move under control in any direction on the court in order to retrieve the shuttle regardless of whether you take one step or a series of steps. To assume this stance, stand alertly facing the net. Spread your feet comfortably with your weight evenly distributed over them. They should be spread just enough to give you freedom of movement and good balance. A good starting point is shoulder width. You can adjust your stance from that position to meet your style and com-

Figure 5.9 Ready position. Stand alertly, spread your feet comfortably with weight evenly distributed over them. Bend your knees slightly, hold the racquet shoulder high, eyes focus on the shuttle.

fort. Bend your knees slightly. This permits you to move instantaneously because the knees must be flexed before you can take a step. Time that you save by cutting down your movements will enable you to get to the shuttle quicker. Flex your hips slightly for the same reason stated above. Hold the racquet slightly in front of you with a forehand grip. The racquet arm is bent at the elbow, and the racquet head is held at least shoulder high. Your eyes should focus on the shuttle to ascertain the direction it will travel.

From this basic stance, you will be able to move quickly into the proper hitting position once you determined where the shuttle is going. All players adjust and vary this stance to meet their own needs. Experiment to find the position best suited for you.

The Strokes

Four basic strokes can be employed to execute all of the various badminton shots. They are the forehand, backhand, overhand, and underhand strokes. The type of stroke that is used during the course of a rally is determined by the flight of the shuttle and the return shot to be hit. Once the latter has been selected, you must then move into the proper hitting stance to execute it.

Forehand

This stroke is used to perform shots on the racquet-hand side of the body. The action of the arm is similar to throwing a ball sidearm. The forehand stroke is used primarily to execute *drive shots* and to return birds that travel at a height between the waist and shoulder. Although the execution of this stroke requires one continuous fluid motion, it is made up of five essential components: the grip, the hitting stance, the backswing, contacting the shuttle, and the follow-through.

Grip. The forehand grip (discussed earlier in this chapter) is used.

Hitting Stance. The most efficient hitting stance for executing forehand shots is to stand sideways facing the sideline. One way to achieve this hitting stance is to simply pivot from the ready position on the foot that is on the same side as your racquet arm. After you pivot, the toes of the pivot foot should point toward the sideline. The other foot swings forward and across your body toward the oncoming shuttle. This foot is adjusted as necessary to compensate for shuttles that travel either too wide or too close to your body. During the pivot, transfer your weight to the pivoting foot. This allows you to make the pivot and then step to meet the approaching shuttle. When time is inadequate for this pattern, a *hop* or *shuffle* into the same stance might be necessary. The sideways stance is preferable and should be used to return shuttles on the forehand side whenever possible.

Backswing. Simultaneously with the pivot, move the racquet arm backward to a position about waist high behind your body. At the same time, rotate your racquet shoulder and hip away from the net. The head of the racquet points upward, and the wrist is cocked. The rotation of the hips and shoulders serves as a windup that enables you to begin a smooth, forward swing. (See Figure 5.10.)

Contacting the Shuttle. To initiate the forward swing, push off the rear foot and step toward the oncoming shuttle. This movement allows for a smooth transfer of weight from the rear to the forward foot. At the moment you contact the shuttle, your body weight should be over the front foot. Immediately following the weight transfer, rotate your hips and shoulders as the racquet swings forward. During the forward swing, the wrist remains cocked and leads the racquet until just before the moment of impact. As the racquet is about to contact the shuttle at a point opposite or slightly in front of the forward hip, snap your wrist, extend your arm fully, and hold the racquet firmly to prevent it from turning or slipping from your hand.

Follow-through. Once the shuttle is contacted, the racquet continues in the intended direction of the shot and then slightly around and away from the body. The weight is shifted entirely over the forward foot, and the rear foot trails to balance the swing.

Figure 5.10 Forehand stroke. Stand facing the sideline with racquet held waist high behind your body . . . rotate shoulders and hips away from net, push off rear foot, step towards shuttle, and swing racquet forward.

Overhand

Of all the strokes, the forehand overhand is relied upon most often and under the greatest variety of conditions. Most players prefer to use this stroke when possible. It is the cornerstone from which a player can build a sound badminton game. The overhand stroke allows you to hit the shuttle *downward,* a necessity for aggressive, power play. It is mainly employed to hit shuttles that are above shoulder level. All of the basic badminton shots needed for successful play can be executed using this stroke, including clear, smash, drop, and push shots. The same fundamentals employed to perform the forehand drive also apply for the forehand-overhand stroke.

Grip.   The forehand grip is used.

Hitting Stance.   From the ready position, pivot into the hitting stance on the foot that is on the same side as your racquet arm. Pivot until you are facing the sideline. Then assume a position similar to a baseball player throwing a ball with an overhand motion. While the rear foot points in the direction of the sideline, the forward foot faces in the direction of the approaching shuttle. In this position, your body weight should rest over your rear foot. (See Figure 5.11.)

Backswing.   As you pivot, swing your racquet arm backwards behind your body. The elbow is bent, and the wrist is cocked. The arm and racquet position is similar to using a back scratcher.

Contacting the Shuttle.   To begin the forward swing, push off from the rear foot and initiate the forward transfer of weight. At the same time, step forward with the front leg and

Figure 5.11 Overhand stroke. Pivot into hitting stance. Rear foot points to sideline while forward foot points toward shuttle. Swing arm backwards . . .   push off rear foot, transferring weight to forward foot. Swing arm forward toward approaching shuttle . . .   after contacting shuttle, the racquet travels down and across your body.

bring the racquet upward toward the shuttle. As the racquet arm moves forward, the elbow leads, followed by the wrist and then the racquet. When the shuttle is contacted, the racquet arm is fully extended and the wrist has been snapped. You literally throw the racquet into the shuttle. Contact is made slightly to the side and in front of your body over your shoulder. To hit the shuttle at its highest point, you must move to a position under it. Mimic an overhand throw. The mechanics are almost identical.

Follow-through.   After the shuttle is hit, the racquet continues to move in the direction of the shot. It then travels down and across your body coming to rest at your side. At the conclusion of the follow-through, your body weight is fully transferred to the forward foot and the back leg trails to maintain balance.

Backhand

This stroke is the twin sister of the forehand and is used to hit shuttles on the nonracquet arm side of the body. Although the major portion of shots are performed on the forehand side of the body, no player's arsenal is complete nor can they experience much success unless they master the backhand stroke.

When first learning the backhand, many players experience difficulty because they do not position themselves correctly or because they lack sufficient strength in the wrist. For these reasons, this stroke requires diligent practice until you can execute it with the same ease that you perform the forehand. If you neglect the backhand in practice, you will pay for it during competitive play. Instead of executing a backhand shot, you will find yourself running around the flight of the oncoming shuttle just to execute a forehand stroke. Sometimes this is neither possible nor practical. It puts a player out of position for the next return and requires time to get in the correct position to make a forehand shot.

Learn how to perform the backhand stroke, or you will be at the mercy of your opponent. Once your adversary learns of your weakness, he or she will take advantage of it by directing shots to your backhand. Nothing is more frustrating than failing to return shuttles that are continually hit to your weak side. Like the forehand, the backhand is one continuous swing composed of five major components—grip, hitting stance, backswing, contacting the shuttle, and follow-through.

Grip.   The recommended grip is the backhand grip described earlier in this chapter. (See Figure 5.4.) However, some players are able to execute the backhand stroke with the same grip they employ for the forehand. On some occasions, you will not have time to change your grip before retrieving a smash or a deceptive, but slower shot. Obviously, you will do well to practice some backhand shots with the forehand grip, regardless of your preference.

Hitting Stance.   The proper position of your body is very important to the correct execution of the backhand stroke. Just as the name implies, when executing this stroke, your back should initially face the net. This is especially true for skilled players when performing a deep backhand stroke. To assume this hitting stance, pivot on the leg opposite the racquet arm. The nonpivot foot is then swung over and across the body toward the side of the approaching shuttle. This foot adjusts for the distance the shuttle is to be played away from your body. During the pivot, your body weight is shifted over the pivoting foot.

Backswing.   Begin your backswing simultaneously as you pivot. Move the racquet to a position behind your body near the shoulder of your nonracquet arm. The elbow of your racquet arm is bent and should point in the direction of the oncoming shuttle. Cock your wrist and point the racquet head in a downward direction. This position will vary somewhat depending on the type of shot you intend to execute. (See Figure 5.12.)

Contacting the Shuttle.   The forward swing is initiated by pushing off the nonracquet foot. The arm swing starts as the hips and shoulders rotate. The elbow leads the way, followed by a rotation of the forearm that causes the racquet face to move into a plane perpendicular to the approach of the shuttle. As contact is made, extend your arm fully and snap your wrist vigorously into the shuttle. During this movement, your body weight is transferred from the rear to the forward foot so that the full power of your body is brought into play. Grasp the handle firmly to prevent it from twisting or slipping.

Follow-through.   Again, as the shuttle leaves the racquet, the swing continues in the direction in which the shuttle is hit. Thus, the follow-through does not swing out to the side but rather toward the intended line of flight of the shuttle. At the completion of the follow-through, your body weight should be over the forward foot.

Underhand

Whenever possible, the shuttle should be contacted high above the net. However, sometimes an underhand stroke must be employed. When a drop shot falls near the net or some other shot cannot be reached soon enough to employ another stroke, use an underhand stroke. Proper execution of this stroke is important when the shuttle cannot be reached above net level. Stroke mechanics are similar to those of the underhand serve. See Chapter 6.

Figure 5.12 Backhand. Move racquet behind your body, cock your wrist . . . | push off the nonracquet foot, rotate hips and shoulders, and swing arm forward toward shuttle . . . | following contact with shuttle, continue racquet swing in the direction of the shot.

Grip. The forehand or the backhand grip may be used in the underhand stroke, depending on which side of your body the stroke will be executed.

Hitting Stance. In this stance, one can face forward or sideways, depending on a player's ability to reach the shuttle. As in the other strokes, your body weight should initially be over the rear foot and your forward foot adjusts for the distance the shuttle is to be hit away from your body.

Backswing. Generally, because of the lack of time, the backswing for the underhand stroke is relatively short. Regardless of how short the backswing is, you should keep your wrist cocked. This will allow you to add power to your stroke, if needed. The most important thing to remember on the backswing is to position your racquet low enough to reach the shuttle before it strikes the floor.

Contacting the Shuttle. Try to contact the shuttle *as early as possible*. For net shots, simply position your racquet and guide the shuttle to the area where you want it to go. When more power is needed to send the shuttle deep into your opponent's court, transfer your body weight from your rear foot to the forward one. This movement together with the wrist snap upon impact with the shuttle will provide sufficient force to hit the shuttle near the baseline on your opponent's side of the court.

Follow-through. The racquet continues up and forward in a full and natural movement when the shot is hit deep in the court. At the end of the follow-through, your body weight should be fully transferred to the forward foot and the racquet should stop in a position over your nonracquet shoulder. For net shots, the follow-through is very short.

Footwork Fundamentals

The importance of good footwork cannot be overstated. It is an essential ingredient for successful play. The ability to execute powerful and well-placed shots is useless unless you can position yourself in the right place on the court and at the right time in relation to the flight of the shuttle. Proper footwork enables you to move quickly and economically about the court into a good position while maintaining your balance and body control. It allows you to have enough time to concentrate and hit an accurate shot even under the most difficult of circumstances. Bad footwork often results in a hurried and poorly timed shot because you are still scrambling to retrieve the bird.

Because the size of the court area that must be covered is small, how fast you run is not what counts. The quickness of your initial movement is what leads to success. This ability to anticipate the coming shot is developed with experience. It can make you seem even quicker than you really are. Ideally, you want to get into a position behind the oncoming shuttle so that you can move toward it to play your shot. To accomplish this, you must be able to move into position, stop, plant your feet, execute the shot, and then return quickly to a good base position to await the return.

Two common errors made by many players are standing flat-footed and not watching the shuttle. If you are one of those players who can hit the shot you want, make the bird travel where you want it to go, and immediately move to a good base position, then there is nothing wrong with your footwork. On the other hand, should you find yourself hurrying and running around the court like a chicken with its head cut off, then your footwork leaves a lot to be desired. However, through hard work, practice, and experience, your footwork can and will improve.

From your base position near the center of the court, you must be able to move instantaneously to intercept the shuttle. To accomplish this, several methods of foot movement may be employed. However, certain foot patterns are better suited than others in a given situation.

The simplest method is *running*. This is a natural movement and need not be taught. It is used to reach shots that fall in front of you or are hit deep in the court. To retrieve these shots, all you do is run or walk to the predetermined spot on the court where you want to contact the shuttle. Forward running is easiest, but one must be careful not to overrun the bird or to crash into the net. Moving backward is slightly more difficult, and two methods of running or walking can be employed. You can either *back pedal* or simply pivot and run or walk to the place where you intend to intercept and strike the shuttle. Back pedaling is running backwards without pivoting. The movement is similar to that employed by a quarterback in football who drops back behind the line to throw a forward pass or a baseball player who runs backwards a short distance to catch a fly ball. In either case, when moving forward or backward, adjust your steps so that you can position yourself behind the shuttle, placing your weight on the rear foot as you plant it on the court. This will put you in a good position to execute your shot.

Shuttles traveling near you on either side can be reached by pivoting and utilizing a *cross-over* step. The pivot is made on the foot on the same side as the approaching shuttle. You then cross or step over the pivoted foot with your other leg in the direction of the oncoming shuttle. The cross-over step is adjusted to give you a balanced stance.

When moving to hit a shuttle near a sideline, a *side-shuffling* or sliding action may be utilized. This movement is employed when only a few steps are necessary to reach the shuttle. It is too slow and awkward to be used when trying to move a great distance across the court. The foot movement involves taking a step with one foot and then moving the other foot up to it, but not past it. The feet are kept parallel and close to the floor. This enables you to move with quick, sliding steps to meet the shuttle. Side-shuffling can also be used to reach shuttles in the fore- or backcourt areas by first pivoting before initiating this movement.

Remember, footwork is a technique in itself and should be mastered. Experiment with the different methods of maneuvering on the court. Practice diligently until footwork becomes a natural part of your game.

6
Serving

Unlike the serve in other racquet sports such as racquetball and tennis, the serve in badminton is primarily a defensive stroke. However, it is still a very important stroke because only the serving side can score points. The serve should not be used simply as a means of putting the bird in play. An effective serve is often the deciding factor that determines the outcome of a game. A good serve helps to build confidence while a poor or ineffective serve can set up your opponent for an outright winner or put you in a vulnerable position from which you may not recover. A weak serve can affect your concentration not only during your serve but also throughout the entire match.

Practice your serves until you develop enough control to put the bird safely in play. Additional practice is required to perfect the various service options. You can practice them either by yourself or with a friend (see Chapter 9 Skill Performance Activities). The true test for finding out how effective your serves are will be in actual competition.

What is considered an effective serve? Any serve your opponent has difficulty in returning is an effective serve! This can be determined by scouting your opponent beforehand to learn your opponent's strengths and weaknesses.

In order to play a respectable game, you should learn to execute four serves. They are the high or deep serve, the low or short serve, the drive, and the flick. (See Figure 6.1.) Each has unique characteristics, and by mixing them up you can keep your opponent off balance trying to anticipate which one you will execute.

Service Positions

Where should you stand while serving? The position the server assumes will vary according to the server's ability and the type of game being played. In singles, the server should stand close to the center line without touching it. The distance you choose to stand from the short service line depends on your ability to move backward and forward with ease to retrieve the return. A good starting point is about three feet from the short service line.

For doubles, the type of doubles system you employ will determine where you stand to initiate the serve. In the side-by-side formation, the server stands about three feet behind the short service line and equidistant from the center and sidelines. Other formations require the server to stand closer to the center line and closer to the short service line. In mixed doubles,

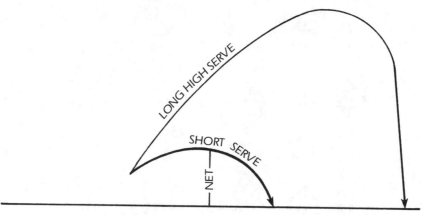

Figure 6.1   Service trajectories.

the man often serves from a deeper position in order to be able to quickly assume the woman-up, man-back formation. Where you actually stand to serve in doubles will depend on your service execution, speed, ability to cover the court, and your partner's abilities.

Holding and Dropping the Bird

To effectuate a good serve, you must hold and drop the bird correctly and consistently. Dropping the bird the same way each time will help you to eliminate some serving errors. It will allow you to contact the bird at the same place every time because the bird will always be dropped at the same distance away from your body. You will need to make no extra body or arm adjustments in order to hit it.

The bird should be held loosely by the skirt or feathers with the cork of the base pointing down toward the floor. Then extend the nonracquet arm comfortably in front and slightly across your body between waist and shoulder height. This permits you to drop the bird well in front of your body to the racquet side. (See Figure 6.2.)

Some advanced players prefer to toss the bird instead of dropping it, especially during singles play. This requires good timing and coordination. It is an advanced technique and is more difficult to master.

The Forehand Serve

Although there are as many and varied styles of serving as there are players, some common factors are present in all of them. Before you add your own personal touch or flair, you should learn and understand the basic factors inherent in each serve.

Grip.   Most serves are executed from the forehand side of the body, utilizing a forehand grip. An important exception is the backhand serve often used in doubles play.

Stance.   Once you assume the correct court position, stand erect and relaxed with your feet spread comfortably apart one in advance of the other. The toes of the forward foot should point toward the net while the rear foot should be positioned at a forty-five degree angle to it, pointing toward the net post. Your knees should be flexed slightly with your body weight over the rear foot. The shoulder of the forward foot should point in the direction the serve is to travel. The bird is held loosely as previously described in advance and to the racquet side of your body between shoulder and waist height.

Racquet Arm. The elbow of the racquet arm is slightly flexed, and the wrist is cocked. Position the racquet behind your body at about waist height. The head of the racquet is level or angles upward.

Forward Swing. As the bird is dropped, swing the racquet forward and simultaneously transfer your body weight to the forward leg. When you contact the bird in front and to the side of your body, snap your wrist for deep serves and maintain the cocked wrist for short serves. (See Figures 6.3 and 6.4.)

Follow-through. After contact is made, the racquet continues forward in the direction the server intends the shuttle to fly. The swing ends in a position over the nonracquet shoulder. The follow-through adds continuity to the swing.

The High Serve

The high serve is generally used in singles play. Ideally, the serve should be hit forcefully so the shuttle travels high and deep and drops vertically near the center of the baseline in the receiving court. A properly executed serve presents the receiver immediately with two problems.

Figure 6.2 High serve. Position racquet waist-high behind your body. Hold the bird loosely by skirt or feathers in front of and to racquet side of body . . .

Figure 6.3 As bird is dropped, swing racquet forward, transfer weight to forward leg . . .

Figure 6.4 Contact the bird in front and to the side of your body, snapping your wrist for a deep serve.

First, it narrows the angle of return. Second, the depth of the serve and the vertical drop limit the type of return shot that can be employed. (See Figure 6.5.)

With this serve, no deception is involved. The intent of the serve is simply to send the shuttle high and deep into your opponent's court. To execute this serve, you may need to take a longer backswing and to add more speed to the forward swing. This allows the wrist to whip through the bird with added power, propelling it high and deep toward the baseline on your opponent's side. It is a very natural serve to execute.

The Low Serve

The primary serve used in doubles is the low serve. The key to its effectiveness is placement. Racquet control, not power, is used to direct the bird's low trajectory as close to the net as possible while hitting it hard enough to barely land in the receiving court. The best place to direct a low serve is an area just beyond the short service line and near the center line in the proper receiving court. This limits the angle of return. Should you find that your opponent has a weak backhand, direct your low serves to that area of the court and force your opponent to return them with the backhand. (See Figure 6.6.)

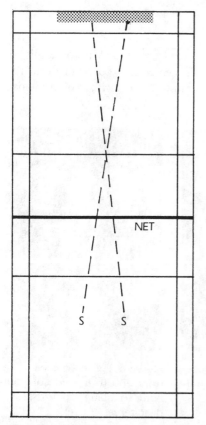

Figure 6.5 High serve placement areas.

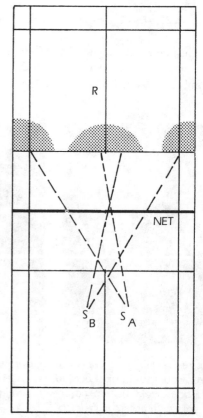

Figure 6.6 Low serve placement areas.
(A) Serving from the right service court.
(B) Serving from the left service court.

The low serve begins with the same preparatory movements as the high serve. However, the forward swing of the racquet is somewhat slower with an emphasis on very little or no wrist action. A transfer of weight forward and a deceptive follow-through toward the desired flight of the bird makes the shot look as much like the long high serve as possible.

The Drive Serve

As the name implies, this serve is hit forcefully with a flat trajectory deep to the back part of your opponent's court. It is an especially effective serve in doubles when used to surprise your opponent on the backhand side. (See Figure 6.7.) Another point of aim is directly at your opponent's chest. This may *jam* your opponent and force an error or a weak return. A poorly executed drive serve can also have an adverse affect. If hit too hard, the bird will travel past the receiving court and you will lose your serve. It's also possible your opponent's racquet will make contact with the bird and the result will be a quick return of the shuttle to your court. This sudden return may catch you off-guard and force an error on your part.

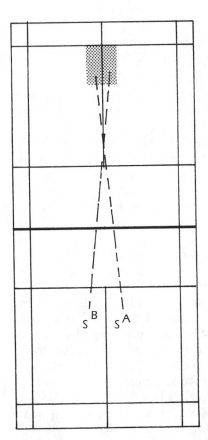

Figure 6.7 Drive serve placement areas. (A) Serve to backhand of right-handed player. (B) Serve to backhand of left-handed player.

Deception is the key to the effectiveness of the drive serve. To execute it, make all the preparatory movements you would make for other serves. Differences to note are: (1) The forward swing is more powerful and faster; (2) The bird is contacted at the highest point allowable by the rules; and (3) More of a sidearm than an underhand swing is used.

The Flick Serve

This serve resembles the movement of a normal low serve except at the last moment when, with a powerful flick (or snap) of your wrist, you send the bird over the head of your aggressive, onrushing opponent. It is a valuable serve when used sparingly against doubles opponents who like to rush the net. Contact with the bird is made somewhere between contact points in the low and high serves. The follow-through is much higher and faster than in the low serve, and the shoulder and forearm play a greater role in the execution of this serve. If your opponent is returning your flick serve quite easily, then you are using it too often, your opponent is standing too deep in the court, or deception is lacking.

The Backhand Low Serve

The backhand low serve is very popular in Southeast Asia and is an excellent serve to master. Although it is used infrequently in the United States, the backhand serve is an important weapon for doubles play. Besides a natural swing, the backhand low serve has several other advantages. It gives your opponent less time to react because the shuttle is contacted in front of your body and closer to the net. The distance the shuttle travels is shorter than in other serves. The shuttle is also more difficult to see because it emanates from and blends in with the white background of your uniform. In addition, you can either hit the low serve at an unusual angle or catch your opponent off guard with a fast flick serve with almost the same motion. All these factors can combine to produce a devastating effect. The backhand is a preferred serve in doubles play. The chief disadvantage is that the server is not in the best position for the return.

Two variations of the backhand serve can be implemented. The first involves a slow pendulumlike swing at the shuttle. The racquet comes through straight, contacting the shuttle full face well in front of the body. Throughout the serve, focus your attention on the shuttle. Only after impact should you lift your head to follow the flight of the bird. (See Figure 6.8.)

The second version involves a *slice* or *chop,* with the racquet face hitting slightly across the shuttle. Once again, watch the shuttle all the way through impact before lifting your head.

For both variations, the stance is square, centered, and as close to the net as is legal. A shortened backhand grip is used with the bird held well out in front of the body just about waist height. This serve can be played with a restricted swing or a simple flick of the wrist with almost the same motion. It can be a simple push, low over the net to drop just in the service court, or a deceptive flick (drive or high serve). Common faults that occur in execution include contacting the shuttle above the waist or having the racquet head above the hand at impact. (See Figure 6.9.)

Figure 6.8 Continue your swing in the direction the shuttle is propelled.

Figure 6.9 Backhand low serve. Stance is square and as close to net as is legal. Use a shortened backhand grip, hold the bird well out in front of your body, waist-high.

. . . flick the wrist . . . or push the bird low over the net.

7
The Shots

The material in Chapter 5 that dealt with basic strokes laid the groundwork necessary for understanding the primary shots presented here. Counting the service, there are seven basic shots in badminton that a player should master. They are the serve, the clear, the drop shot, the smash, the drive, the round-the-head, and the net shot. Although all of these require time and practice for proficiency, students of the game should become familiar with them and begin to employ each at the earliest opportunity.

As you study the explanations on shot making, refer to Figures 7.1, 7.4, and 7.10, which illustrate the trajectories of the various shots. The instruction is organized according to court areas from which particular shots will usually be taken. This integration of information on trajectories, strategies, and mechanics will help speed your learning.

Shots from Near the Back Boundary

Trying to hit a smash from the baseline is almost always counterproductive in singles play. The rapid deceleration of the shuttle over the long distance, coupled with the extra time that it takes to regain the base position after this powerful shot, gives your opponent an advantage. It is generally better to hit either a defensive clear or a drop shot, disguising your intent until the last split second. (See Figure 7.1.)

The Forehand-Overhand Defensive Clear

Most players find this shot easier to control than either the underhand or the backhand-overhand clears. The similarity of stroke execution also makes this a very deceptive shot because your opponent does not know whether you are going to hit a clear, a drop, or a smash. The mechanics are almost identical to those of throwing a ball. In preparation for hitting this shot, one must get into position quickly and assume a sideways stance with your nonracquet shoulder pointing toward the net as you face the sideline. Grasp the racquet with a forehand grip, and swing it behind your body as if to hit a smash. The elbow of your racquet arm should be flexed with the racquet pointing to the side and slightly downward. The hand grasping the racquet handle is close to your ear, and the wrist is cocked. Your body weight should be over the rear foot while your nonracquet arm points toward the oncoming shuttle. This serves sev-

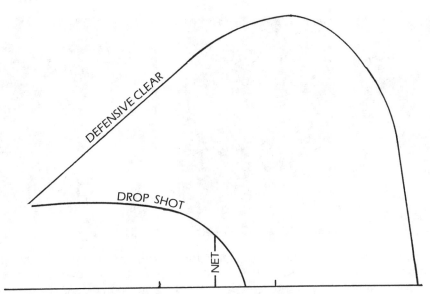

Figure 7.1 Shot trajectories from near the boundary line.

eral purposes. It helps with your balance, encourages shoulder rotation, and assists in sighting the shuttle. Later on, if you can achieve good shoulder rotation without the pointing, you may choose to omit it.

The forward swing begins by pushing off the back foot. Swing the racquet forward and up in a throwing motion as you transfer your body weight to the front foot. With the weight shift, there is a strong hip rotation followed by a shoulder rotation toward the net. The racquet arm then straightens, and the wrist snaps just before the racquet impacts the shuttle. Contact is made at the highest point possible above the head (consistent with comfort—don't strain), slightly in front of your body. Never, never let the shuttle get past your head. The racquet face is flat at the normal point of impact. In order to hit the bird with a flat face, inward wrist rotation occurs during the wrist snap. To get the desired trajectory, the racquet face must be aimed somewhat upward. After striking the shuttle, the racquet continues forward and up along the line of flight of the bird as long as possible and then down to a position about waist high on the opposite side of your body. (See Figure 7.2.)

The primary purposes of this shot are to buy time, force your opponent deep in the court, and limit the possible return shots. This not only allows you time to move or return to a good base position but also gives you added resting time between returns because of the long flight time the shuttle takes to traverse the court. The opportunity to rest is very important to players who are not as physically fit as their opponents or during extended rallies. A well-placed clear hit to your opponent's weakness can be a most effective shot. It can either force an outright error or elicit a weak return that will set you up for an easy smash.

For the clear to be effective, it must be hit deep and high so that the bird will fall perpendicular to the floor near the back boundary line, preferably in your opponent's backhand corner of the court. Otherwise, the shuttle may be returned quickly with a powerful smash or a

Figure 7.2 Overhand stroke. Pivot into hitting stance. Rear foot points to sideline while forward foot points toward shuttle. Swing arm backwards . . .

push off rear foot, transferring weight to your forward foot . . . swing arm forward toward approaching shuttle . . .

after contacting shuttle, the racquet travels down and across your body.

deceptive and delicate drop. A correctly executed defensive clear will land within one foot of your opponent's baseline. To accomplish this, a powerful stroke is necessary to move the bird the entire length of the court. When the air resistance finally stops the upward and forward momentum of the shuttle, the final part of the pathway is almost vertically downward, taxing the skill and power of your opponent to the utmost. Returning a clear with a smash from deep in the court requires much power. Very few players can smash effectively from deep in the court because the speed of the shuttle is greatly diminished by the time it passes over the net. Also, a downward smash is not possible from a position deep in the back court.

Lastly, the defensive clear is the safest and most frequently used of the basic shots hit during a rally, especially in singles play. It can truly be referred to as the "workhorse" of badminton. Practice it diligently because it is a very important component of the game.

The Backhand-Overhand Defensive Clear

This is one of the most difficult shots to execute properly. It is the one your opponent will attempt to force you to hit. The action involved in making this shot is very similar to that used to flick a towel at a target on a ceiling that you can barely reach. To execute it, you should face the sideline with feet comfortably spread, sideways to the net. The shoulder of your racquet arm points to the net. The stance is almost exactly opposite of that employed for the forehand. Hold the racquet with the backhand grip, and position it so that the racquet head is over your nonracquet shoulder. This is similar to a back-scratching position. The elbow of the racquet arm is flexed and should point upwards toward the oncoming shuttle. As you backswing, turn your hips slightly so your back is exposed to the net. Your knees should be flexed slightly with your body weight over the rear or nonracquet foot. In this position, you should feel as if your body were coiled like a spring ready to be unleashed at the proper moment. As you become more skilled, you may be able to hit a backhand clear from a position facing a rear corner of the court or even the back boundary line.

The primary objective of your swing is to contact the shuttle at a point immediately above the shoulder of your racquet arm. As you see the shuttle approach this spot, whip the racquet head forward and upward to contact it. Your elbow should lead the arm movement from the very start of the racquet motion, followed by the forearm with the wrist still cocked. The racquet, pointed downward at the onset of the weight shift, is *pulled* upward. As your arm extends, snap the racquet head vigorously at and through the shuttle. Contact should be made when your arm is fully extended and the racquet face is square. The extension or flick of your wrist should be clearly in an upward as opposed to a forward or outward direction. The hand then stops when the arm is in a vertical position. This latter point is perhaps the most important key in developing the coordinated skill and power necessary for executing this difficult shot. The tendency is to sweep the whole arm through, trying to generate adequate power. This is counterproductive. The only way to build up the necessary racquet speed and subsequent power is with the towel-flick move, stopping the hand at the vertical in the racquet follow-through. The follow-through is really negligible in this stroke because the elbow will lock at the moment of impact. Remember, the major keys to the successful and easy execution of this shot are timing and a vigorous wrist flick. These two factors are extremely important, and one without the other will not suffice. This is a very difficult shot to make from deep in the court. Before attempting it from near the back boundary line, spend time perfecting the mechanics from an area closer to the net. As you coordinate the different parts of the stroke perfectly, gradually move deeper in the court. (See Figure 7.3.)

Figure 7.3 Backhand-overhand defensive clear. Face the sideline. Shoulder of racquet arm points to the net, elbow of racquet arm is flexed, and points upward toward shuttle . . . racquet head points downward.

. . . contact is made when arm is fully extended. Wrist flick should be upward, hand stops when arm is in vertical position, and follow-through is negligible.

Should you have difficulty in making an effective clear when playing it overhead, you can modify the stroke by letting the shuttle drop lower before contacting it. The actual point of impact will then occur at a height somewhere between the waist and head. Regardless of where contact is made, getting your racquet underneath it is extremely important. Take a big swing, and hit the shuttle at arm's length. When making a backhand clear in this manner, note that a long backswing and a full arm extension upon impact are essential for power. Contacting the shuttle too close to the body cramps the action of the swing, and a premature striking of the shuttle before a full racquet swing prevents you from imparting the needed force to make the bird travel both high and deep to your opponent's side of the court. This stroke requires less technique in timing and wrist action than the standard clear but more physical effort. In this stroking movement, the elbow does not actually point upward. However, it still points in the direction of the oncoming shuttle and leads the arm action as in the overhand-backhand clear movement previously discussed. The foot movement, hip rotation, and weight transfer are also the same. The follow-through of the racquet arm continues on a natural path upward in the intended direction of the path of the shuttle and then down and to the racquet side of the body. The swinging motion should be continuous so as not to impede the speed and flight of the shuttle.

The Drop Shot

The drop is a finesse shot. It is a soft, delicate shot that requires timing and control. As an alternative to the clear from the back boundary line, the drop shot is played either straight ahead or crosscourt. When executed correctly, the shuttle travels just above the net into the forecourt of your opponent. Preparation for the drop should resemble the clear and the smash right up to the moment of impact to create the deception necessary to make it effective. Always try to look as if you are going to hit one of the other strokes.

The preparatory movements are similar in appearance to those described for the overhand clear or smash (i.e., grip, footwork, body rotation, and racquet action) until just prior to contacting the shuttle. As you swing the racquet forward, slow the arm and wrist action just before impact and perform only a slight follow-through to give added *feel* to the shot. Slowing the arm and wrist movement tends to deaden the impact. This slow-arm action is better than stopping the forearm at the vertical because it allows for more control. The shuttle should be met in front of your body with the arm fully extended. The racquet face is not tilted slightly upward as in the clear but is slightly closed at the moment of impact and almost perpendicular to the floor. The arm action employed may be described as a push with the whole arm. This shot lacks the power of a clear or a smash and results in slow flight of the bird. The follow-through is slight but aimed exactly at the spot where you wish the shuttle to cross over the net. Since *touch,* not power, is the essence of the drop, little wrist action is necessary.

An alternative way of making the drop is to use more wrist snap but to keep the racquet face open, resulting in a slice, or *cut drop.* The slicing action is very effective in reducing the power and changing the direction of flight. Learn different degrees of wrist and arm dominance. This will allow you to execute the flatter fast drops used in doubles as well as the slow *coconut drop,* so named for the path of flight after the shuttle crosses the net. The *fast drop* is planned to pass the net player and force an upward stroke by the back player. The slow drop is not well hit unless it lands between the net and short service line, maximizing pressure on the defensive player.

Alternating drops with clears is an excellent way to test your opponent's endurance. However, you must be careful not to overdo the drop. Employ it wisely as a companion shot to the clear and smash, but too-frequent use will minimize its value. The margin of error for a poorly executed drop is severe. Even accurately placed drop shots are often intercepted and returned. This is a result of the slow nature of the shuttle's flight. Unfortunately, any shuttle hit slowly will allow your opponent time to move into position to retrieve it. Always keep in mind that the key to successful execution of the drop shop is deception.

The Backhand Drop Shot

Like the forehand drop shot, successful execution of the backhand drop shot depends on disguising it. The shot must be made to look like you are hitting a clear or a smash. This type of deception will force your opponent to momentarily hold base position before anticipating where the shuttle will be hit. The early preparation stages for shot execution are identical to both the backhand clear and smash. The main difference is the slowing down of the racquet prior to impact and the checking of the wrist. The crosscourt backhand drop shot tends to be easier to execute because of the natural swing of the stroke. However, one should also learn the straight drop. The decision of when to employ this shot depends on your ability and your relation to your opponent's position on the court.

The Midcourt Shots

While it is true that defensive clears and drop shots can be made from midcourt, more often the following shots should be hit—the smash, the drive, and the attacking clear. The choice of shot depends somewhat on your opponent's court position, but more significantly on the height at which you can make contact with the shuttle. A high bird calls for the smash. If the shuttle is at or above net level, but too low to smash, the drive shot is ideal. Two shots that can be used when the shuttle falls below tape level are the attacking or the defensive clears. (See Figure 7.4.)

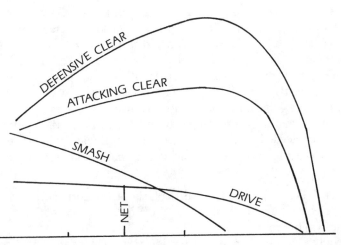

Figure 7.4 Shot trajectories from near midcourt.

The Smash

This shot is the principal rally winner in badminton. It is a spectacular and powerful over-head shot that is akin to the touchdown bomb in football, the home run in baseball, and the kill in racquetball. Although the smash can be played from anywhere in the court, it is generally executed from midcourt in the area between the doubles back and front service lines.

The smash is hit with an overhand stroke, usually from the forehand side. The shuttle should be contacted high above your head and hit forcefully so it angles downward to an un-protected area of the court. Even though speed is a valuable component of the shot, place-ment is equally, if not more, important. Hitting the shuttle to an unprotected area of the court makes it even more difficult to return.

For best results, make sure you contact the shuttle as high overhead as possible with the racquet face angled downward at the point of contact. When the shuttle travels at a steep an-gle, it is extremely difficult to return. The angle of contact depends on your court position. The closer you are to the net, the steeper the angle, and vice-versa. The farther you are away from the net, the flatter the angle to the floor. Speed, which is another important component of the smash, diminishes greatly over longer distances. This, coupled with the flat trajectory, makes the return of smashes executed from near the baseline easier for the receiver.

Forehand Smash. To execute an effective smash, move quickly into position. Attempt to disguise the stroke, preparing as though you were planning to hit a drop or a clear. The fore-hand smash is an overhand stroke performed with the nonracquet arm facing the net. The rac-quet arm is positioned behind the body with the elbow bent and wrist cocked. The handle of the racquet is held firmly with the forehand grip, especially at the moment of impact. Body weight should be initially over the rear foot. As the bird approaches, step toward it and trans-fer your weight to the stepping or forward foot. Immediately following this movement, rotate your hips and shoulders and swing the racquet to contact the shuttle at the highest point. The follow-through of the swing continues down and in the direction the shuttle is hit. (See Figure 7.5.)

Power is added to the shot by a vigorous snapping of the wrist just prior to impact. The wrist snap is made with a simultaneous inward rotation, making the racquet face square when the shuttle is contacted. The forceful wrist snap and correct timing of the hit are essential to impart the necessary high velocity to the shuttle.

When learning to perform the smash, start slowly. Practice both your timing and tech-nique. As these components improve, increase the speed of your swing. Eventually you will develop a powerful stroke—one that you can confidently enjoy and rely on during play.

After you learn the smash, be careful not to overuse it. Learn the other strokes equally well because the effort needed to perform the smash continually will cause you to fatigue quickly. However, when the shuttle is above the net and in your forecourt, by all means, "Smash it!"

Backhand Smash. This is an extremely difficult shot to perform correctly. Very few play-ers can efficiently execute it unless the shuttle is close to the net. It is definitely not a shot you should hit from deep in the court.

The preparation to hit a backhand smash is identical to that for a backhand clear except the wrist is snapped downward instead of upward. Since it is necessary to get the racquet above the shuttle to accomplish this flicking action, you should contact the bird about a foot in front of you and close to the sideline. The vigorous wrist snap and outward wrist rotation make the racquet face square with the shuttle when it is contacted. They also allow for a more pronounced follow-through and enable you to get the racquet on top of the shuttle.

Jumping Smash.   A final variation of the smash that is occasionally used by athletic, fit, and skilled players is the jumping smash shot. By jumping, you can make the shot from a height that allows an even steeper angle. Coordination of the jump and stroke is not easy, and the extra time needed for regaining balance and the base position is a problem. Despite the disadvantages, it can be a satisfying, productive, and spectacular shot when carried out properly. (See Figure 7.6.)

To perform a jumping smash, you employ the same mechanics and techniques used to hit a nonjumping smash. The main difference is timing your jump to have your racquet swing contact the shuttle at the highest point with maximum power. Timing the hit is critical to successful execution. If you are not in good physical condition, you may find this shot fatiguing. Employ this shot judiciously. If you have not practiced it, then do not attempt it in competition. The perfect execution of this shot is an advanced technique used only by highly skilled players.

Smash Shot Summary.   The instructions for hitting a smash should be familiar to you since they are the same patterns employed in the first phases for executing forehand and backhand clears and drop shots. All of these strokes should be executed in the same way for two reasons: (1) For grooving patterns, learning a single move is faster than learning different patterns for each stroke and (2) your opponent cannot determine what stroke to anticipate until the last split second before you make contact with the bird. Differentiating both forehand and

Figure 7.5   Forehand smash. Non-racquet arm should face the net. Position your body with weight over rear foot . . .

contact the shuttle at highest point, and snap wrist vigorously. Follow-through of swing continues down and in direction the shuttle is hit.

Figure 7.6 Jump smash. Timing is critical, and technique is similar to nonjumping smash shots.

backhand smashes from clears, you hit the bird further out in front (one to two feet, depending on your distance from the net) of your body, and the racquet is clearly on top of the shuttle, ensuring a sharp, downward flight. The downward angle is probably at least as important as the speed with which the shuttle is hit. In fact, sometimes it is better to take a little off the power to make sure that you can completely control the shot. This is particularly true for beginners.

Advanced players often choose to slacken the speed of the smash for several reasons: (1) To avoid hitting or timing errors when making contact with the shuttle; (2) to maintain more control of the shuttle's flight, taking advantage of placement opportunities when your opponent is out of position, and (3) to be able to regain balance and move to a good base position faster.

One way of reducing the power and speed of the smash is to make the stroke with the racquet face slightly open. This will produce the deceptive *cut smash*.

The Drive

Hit with either a forehand or backhand stroke, the drive is an offensive, flat sidearm shot used to hit shuttles that are close to tape height but have dropped too low to smash and yet not so low that you want to play an upward defensive stroke. Ideally, the bird should be contacted about shoulder level and directed in a fairly flat trajectory as parallel to the floor as possible. If hit correctly, the bird will barely skim over the net in a horizontal plane. Generally, it is aimed *down the line* toward the back boxes or straight at your opponent's racquet side.

The drive shot is mainly used in doubles and mixed doubles but can be employed in singles, especially when a quick placement is needed, your opponent is out of position, or you want to hurry your opponent. In doubles, it is extremely effective against the up-and-back formation of play and is often hit by the back player. When hit directly at your opponent as a quick return, it may force a weak reply or an error. Drive shots hit to the vulnerable or open spots on the court often result in outright winners. The drive is an effective attack stroke ranking second only to the smash.

Forehand Drive.   This stroke employs a swing similar to throwing a ball sidearm or throwing the racquet at the bird in the widest possible arc. The foot position is identical to the other forehand strokes (i.e., sideways to the net). However, you may also employ the drive shot while facing the net. In this position, the shuttle may be contacted beside the racquet foot. For some players, this is a more natural stance. It provides a greater reach, allows one to get to the shuttle quickly and allows faster recovery to a good base position. (See Figure 7.7.)

Strike the shuttle with the full face of the racquet at arm's length, slightly in front of your body at approximately net height. The racquet should be held firmly with a forehand grip. When hitting off the racquet foot, your body should lean into the shot. Otherwise, use the same mechanics as discussed for the other forehand shots—weight over the rear leg, step toward the approaching shuttle, transfer weight, and so on. The only disadvantage of the racquet-foot-forward stance is that less power can be generated because the body rotates less. However, it is recommended primarily because of the time saved getting into hitting position and back to the base position.

Figure 7.7 Forehand drive. The armswing is similar to throwing a ball sidearm. Contacting the shuttle to the side of racquet foot allows you to get to shuttle quickly.

. . . strike with full face of racquet at arm's length, slightly in front of body when hitting off racquet foot.

Your wrist should uncock just prior to contacting the bird and only to the degree necessary to determine the path of it. If the shuttle is directed down the line, hit the bird slightly in front of your body with the arms and shoulders doing most of the work. For crosscourt shots, the shuttle should be contacted twelve to eighteen inches in front of your body. Utilize more wrist snap to provide final impetus in the direction you want the shuttle to travel. Whether down the line or crosscourt, hit the shuttle firmly and keep the racquet face perpendicular to the shuttle's line of flight. Also, to hit the shot correctly and achieve maximum power, make sure the bird does not travel too close to your body, cramping your stroke. The follow-through continues forward and out in the direction the bird is hit before the racquet moves across your chest to the opposite shoulder. For drives hit straight down the line, the follow-through is more abbreviated than for those hit crosscourt.

Backhand Drive.   The exact reverse of the forehand drive is the backhand drive shot. To execute it, move your feet into position outlined for the backhand clear (i.e., facing the sideline). Hold the racquet firmly, employing the backhand grip. The thumb is placed on the flat portion of the racquet handle to give added support and snap as needed. However, when time is of the essence, no change in grips is necessary.

The arm is brought back to a position where the racquet hand is almost touching the opposite shoulder. The wrist is cocked, and your elbow points toward the approaching shuttle, parallel to the floor. The forward swing is initiated by an extension of the elbow, straightening the arm. The wrist then uncocks and rotates outward toward the little finger just before impact, causing a flat racquet face to strike the shuttle diagonally in front of the forward foot.

The follow-through follows the shuttle's line of flight and then falls naturally around to the racquet side of your body. This helps to position your body squarely to the net in a good ready stance to await the potential return. (See Figure 7.8.)

Around-the Head.   As the name implies, the around-the-head is an overhead shot played with the forehand face of the racquet above and around the head on the backhand side of the body. This unusual stroke is peculiar to badminton and can be used to hit a smash, a drop, or a clear on the backhand side. It is frequently substituted for the backhand because it can equate the full power of the forehand. The around-the-head shot can also be used defensively against a drive serve to the backhand side. In other situations, it can be used offensively to achieve more power.

The execution of the around-the-head is very similar to other overhand strokes. The main differences are stance (facing the net) and contact point (over the nonracquet shoulder). When performing this stroke, assume a stance facing the net. Your feet should be parallel and spread slightly wider than for a normal forehand stroke in order to maintain your balance. Move the racquet to a back-scratching position behind the body as in the clear. Arch your back and bend sideways toward your nonracquet arm. Do not lean too far back because this can strain the muscles of your back. Move the racquet up, back, and then over the top of your head as your shoulders rotate. The forehand face of the racquet should meet the shuttle at a point beyond your nonracquet shoulder. During the stroke, the upper arm almost touches the right ear and the forearm barely clears the top of the head. (See Figure 7.9.)

The follow-through will be determined by the type of shot executed. However, regardless of the shot, the racquet should continue in the same direction as the shuttle. At the end of the follow-through, your body weight should be over your racquet foot. Once again, the wrist plays a vital role in effective shot execution. A crisp wrist snap into the shuttle is important to compensate for the lack of body weight applied to the shot. After hitting the shuttle, the tendency is to overbalance to the nonracquet side. This overbalancing will be more pronounced the farther away from you the shot is played. Therefore, after executing the around-the-head shot, concentrate on a rapid recovery. If not, you will have difficulty in getting into a good position to await the return shot.

Lastly, do not overplay this shot. The twisting of the body and the extra footwork needed to move into position to hit the shuttle and recover will cause you to tire more rapidly. However, the around-the-head is a more aggressive shot than the backhand and can be effective at the appropriate opportunity. While this is not your prettiest shot, it is a valuable part of every good player's arsenal of weapons.

Attacking Clear.   Actually, both the attacking and the defensive clears can be important shots executed from midcourt. We have already presented the mechanics of the defensive clear earlier in this chapter, so only the attacking clear, which is perhaps used more frequently from the midcourt area, will be discussed here. The attacking clear can be hit forehand or backhand, employing mechanics similar to those used to perform the defensive clear except that the bird is contacted slightly more in front of the body with the racquet face nearing the vertical. The resulting trajectory is relatively flat. The bird is struck with sufficient speed and height so that it will pass just out of your opponent's reach. Naturally, with a lower trajectory

Figure 7.8 Backhand drive. Face the sideline with your arm positioned so that the racquet hand is almost touching your opposite shoulder, wrist cocked . . .

strike the shuttle with a flat racquet face, diagonally in front of forward foot. Follow-through continues in the shuttle's line of flight.

Figure 7.9 Around-the-head. Face the net with your racquet positioned behind your body in a back-scratching position . . .

the racquet moves up, back, and over across the top of your head, and meets the shuttle at a point beyond your nonracquet shoulder . . .

the follow-through continues in the same direction as the shuttle. At the end of the follow-through, weight is over the racquet foot.

the shuttle falls more quickly, allowing your opponent less time to retrieve the bird. Since the arc is flatter, the stroke requires controlled execution. Birds hit too hard will go out of play, and ones hit too soft will result in an easy return. For successful execution, control your power because the bird must be hit precisely, with enough force to pass your opponent yet delicately so that the shuttle will stay in the court. This type of clear is usually hit when your opponent is off balance or too far forward, perhaps anticipating a drop shot or following a well-placed drop shot. Whenever you make this shot with your opponent out of position, move up in the court in anticipation of a weak return. Sometimes the attacking clear is hit for an outright winner; more often the ensuing shot is the one you can put away for an easy point.

Shots from Near the Net

Shots from up close, near the net, are most exciting! Decisions must be made quickly, and shot selection and execution are critical.

Those shots taken in the area from the short service line to the net are referred to as *net shots*. Execution of net shots is a fine art, with choices ranging from the more defensive underhand clear to the delicately played hairpin. When executing net shots, always try to keep in mind that the shuttle should be contacted as high and as close to the top of the net as possible. However, the lower a shot is played, the more difficult it is to return effectively. Net shots hit from below net level include the hairpin, the crosscourt, and the underhand clear. Those attempted from above the net are the smash and the push, or dab. (See Figure 7.10.)

To perform a net shot, move to a position close to the net but not so close as to restrict your movement. Being too close to the net leaves your backcourt area susceptible to attacks, especially in singles play. From an appropriate position, execute the net shot dictated by your opponent's position and movement.

If you can approach the net for a weak return and take advantage by hitting a sharply down-angled, well-placed smash or tap, you have no particular problem. But, if your foe has made a drop shot that is hard to get to and you have to play a shot while noting your opponent's court movement and position with your peripheral vision, the options are generally few. You can play an underhand clear, the value of which will largely be determined by how low and how close to the net you must make contact. You also have the choice of making an answering drop shot, either straight or crosscourt. Review the fundamentals of the underhand stroke in Chapter 5.

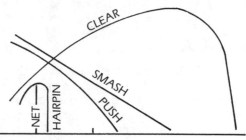

Figure 7.10 Shot trajectories from near the net.

To execute net shots, the racquet is usually held loosely in the fingers to allow for more touch. The feet, body, and upper arm are used primarily for reaching the shuttle. The actual shot is performed with the forearm, the wrist, and the hand. The movement of the wrist may be controlled as in the hairpin crosscourt and push, or it may be vigorous as in the clear, push, or smash. Only the attack shots need explosive power; the others require touch and control.

The follow-through for each shot should always be in the direction in which you want the shuttle to go. Sometimes you may have to guide the shuttle and at other times your follow-through may be abbreviated or extended. The nature of the shot will dictate it.

Underhand Clear. The defensive answer to a shuttle hit low in the net area is the underhand clear. Proper execution of it will allow you time to return to a good base position after retrieving a drop or one of the other net shots.

When retrieving a net shot, the racquet foot should be forward in both the backhand and forehand shots regardless of whether or not you execute a clear or a drop. This gives you a longer reach and thus allows you to get to the bird quicker. The success of the underhand clear is tied to the relationship of the bird to the net. If the bird is very close to the net and you must hit it from near the floor, you will not be able to clear deep and must quickly defend an inevitable, tough offensive shot such as a smash or an attacking clear. In these cases, your only useful option is to decide how to place a drop shot. If you can use the underhand clear, you will nearly always desire a defensive trajectory that will allow you to gain time to recover. However, if you can contact the shuttle fairly high and your opponent is close to the net, an attacking (lower trajectory) clear might be possible. The mechanics of the shot are almost exactly like those of the high, deep serve used in singles play except that on the net shots the racquet foot is usually forward. For both forehand and backhand shots, the body is rotated away from the net and the wrist is cocked while moving into position. As the stroke commences, hip and shoulder rotation toward the net is followed by racquet action. The racquet makes an underhand sweeping arc with the wrist snapping just prior to contact. In the backhand stroke, the elbow leads the racquet. For both, the follow-through is high and followed by an immediate move back to the base position. When shuttles are hit from relatively high positions near the top of the net, care must be taken, especially when the attacking clear is used, not to generate so much power that you overshoot the back boundary line. Conversely, shots made from a very low position should be aimed high for a defensive clear, employing as much wrist snap and power as possible.

Harpin Net Shot. The hairpin net shot receives its name from the flight pattern of the shuttle. It travels straight up, over, and straight down, falling perpendicular to the floor and close to the net on your opponent's side of the court. The distance the shuttle travels is the least of any of the shots. (See Figures 7.10 and 7.11.)

In order to get to the bird quickly, use the racquet-foot-forward approach. The combined movements of the footwork and the racquet action have been compared to the thrust in fencing. The racquet head is almost parallel to the floor, perhaps slightly tipped toward the net if you are not too close to it. For both backhand and forehand net shots, using the standard backhand and forehand grips, the shuttle is caressed rather than hit over the net. A hit will result in a too high return that will usually be killed. The gentle caress will tumble the bird over the net so low that your opponent's choices are few. The wrist is cocked throughout, the backswing is nil, and the entire stroke usually takes place in less than a foot of racquet movement. Very minimal arm or wrist movement is required to perform this shot, and only a minimum of follow-through is recommended. The racquet face directs the shuttle with a slight movement in that direction. Some last minute wrist action may be necessary if you wish to crosscourt your hairpin or if you decide at the last second that your opponent is so close to the net that a clear is called for. The ideal drop shot from near the net exhibits a softness of touch that gently guides the shuttle's trajectory so close to the net and with such finesse that it will barely float over the tape and tumble straight down, unplayable by your opponent.

Crosscourt Net Shot.   A variation of the hairpin is the crosscourt or *angle net shot,* as it is sometimes called. In this shot, the shuttle travels across the court toward the opposite net post. As in the hairpin net shot, the shuttle should barely skim the top of the net as it passes over it. Otherwise, it will result in an easy setup, and your opponent will quickly pounce on it for a winner. (See Figure 7.12.)

The angle of the face of the racquet determines how close the bird will fly near the net. Ideally, you would like the shuttle to travel as long as possible on your side of the court until it

Figure 7.11 Hairpin net shot. With your racquet foot forward and the racquet almost parallel to floor, contact the shuttle at highest point possible . . . backswing is minimal; "caress" the bird over the net.

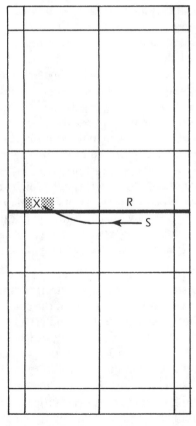

Figure 7.12 Crosscourt net shot placement area.

reaches within a foot or two of the sideline. Then the shuttle passes over the net and drops into your opponent's court for a winner or a difficult return. As the shuttle approaches, watch it until it contacts the racquet strings. With a firm pushing action, direct the bird upward and outward crosscourt to the spot you have chosen. Owing to the distance the shuttle will travel, this shot is easier to control than other net options.

Push, or Dab, Net Shot.   All shuttles that can be played above and near the net should be hit in a downward direction. This shot known as the push or dab is performed mainly with a wrist flick. Very little backswing, if any, is required. (See Figure 7.13.)

Figure 7.13 Push or dab shot. This shot is performed mainly with a flick of the wrist. Hit the shuttle downward.

Backhand Net Shot.   All the net shots performed with the forehand can also be executed from the backhand side. The hairpin and the crosscourt can be gently pushed when the shuttle is near the top of the net or lifted from below it. Vigorous clears utilizing the techniques described earlier in this chapter can also be employed.

Smash Net Shot.   The most important attack shot played above net level is the smash. It is the best and most effective return of a high, short shot. When the opportunity presents itself, do not hesitate to use it. However, be careful that your swing does not go into the net. For more information regarding this shot, review the previous discussion of the smash earlier in this chapter.

Shot Placement Summary

Now that you understand the mechanics, strategies, and trajectories of the various shots, let us summarize the final dimension, shot placement. Although this was covered to a degree in the preceding sections, it is important enough to merit additional attention. Examine Figures 7.14, 7.15, 7.16, and 7.17, and analyze the presentations of strategic target areas for each particular shot. Keep in mind that for all general rules, exceptions exist. In most cases, however, these are the winning patterns.

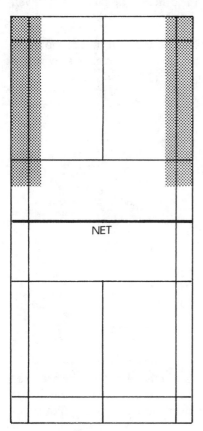

Figure 7.14 Target areas for drive shots and smash shots. Hit the bird near the side boundaries of the court.

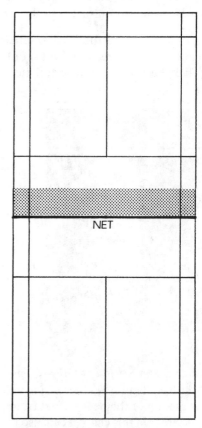

Figure 7.15 Target area for hairpin and drop shots. Hit the bird so that it barely clears the net and lands as close to the net as possible.

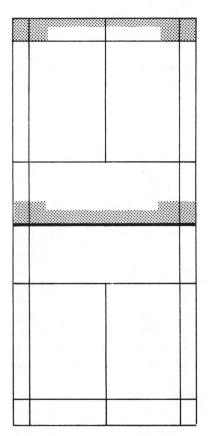

Figure 7.16 Target areas of the masters.

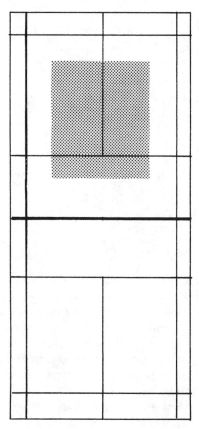

Figure 7.17 Target area to be avoided.

8
Strategy

General

Choosing Your Style

Basically, two styles of play are primarily used in badminton. They are the running, defensive game and the power, offensive method of play. The former requires a player to be in excellent physical condition because the rallies are quite long, while the latter is a more spectacular, aggressive, gambling style of play. Players who specialize in the defensive game usually employ the high serve followed mostly by drops and defensive clears. On the other hand, the attacking player must master and employ a mixture of serves combined with a variety of shots such as smashes, cut smashes, fast drops, and attacking clears.

Although you must select and develop a style of play that suits your own temperament and physical abilities, make sure that your game play is flexible enough to meet the challenges of your opponents. When playing a contest, keep the following two points in mind: (1) Play your game according to your own strengths and abilities (never according to your opponent's), and (2) change your style of play *only* if you are losing (never when you are winning).

Regardless of the type of strategy you wish to employ, you will have difficulty implementing it unless you master the skills and techniques vital to successful badminton play. An intelligent and analytical approach combined with effective skill execution is essential. Without the ability to analyze your opponent's strengths and weaknesses so you can apply your own skills opportunistically, the time spent planning your strategy will be worthless. Badminton is clearly a thinking player's game. Knowing when and where to hit a shot is often more effective than brute force or forced shots.

Patience Versus Aggression

A key to successful badminton play can be summed up in the words *patient aggressiveness*. At first, this might appear to be a contradiction in terms. However, success in badminton combines ability to know what shot to hit, when to execute it, and the patience to wait until the right time during the course of a rally before employing it. Many times inexperienced players try to force shots or to attempt ones beyond their skill level.

For example, the smash is best used to end a rally. It should not be used indiscriminantly, especially when conditions are not right. The temptation to hit a smash regardless of one's position on the court is great because it is the most stunning and sensational badminton shot. However, both overuse and poor court position can adversely affect its success ratio.

Vary your play. Do not be predictable. Use deception. Disguise your shots. Keep your opponent deep in the court and on the move. But most of all, be patient. Remember, good things come to those who wait.

By mixing up your shots and making your opponent run, you will eventually elicit a weak return. When this occurs, your moment is at hand. Take advantage of it. Put the bird away for a winner with a well-placed, powerful smash. Such is the reward of the patient, aggressive player.

Winners Hit Early and Downward

Players who are continually forced during a rally to hit the shuttle upward generally lose. The objective of your shots should be to cause weak returns so that you can move into position to hit the bird downward mercilessly and aggressively.

Even while practicing or warming up, avoid sloppy play. As the bird drops, move quickly into position and contact it as soon as you can reach it. This will allow you to execute more drives and smashes. By hitting the shuttle at its highest point, you shorten the distance the bird travels, thus decreasing the amount of time your opponent has to rest and react between shots. The sooner and higher you contact the bird, the less taxing it is physically because you do not need as much strength to hit the bird over the net. This is particularly important in net play. Hitting the bird as early as possible during net play permits more pushes and taps downward. It also makes hairpins and drops more deadly. Stopping the shuttle high and early with an almost motionless racquet, by pushing, brushing, or tumbling the bird barely over the net is very rewarding. If you choose to clear, taking the shuttle early improves your angle immeasurably, bettering your chances of making a deep shot.

Lines, Gaps, and Angles

You can beat yourself by being overly ambitious in aiming at the side- and base-lines. The penalty for missing your target is too great. Leave yourself a safe margin for error while at the same time allowing your opponent a chance to make mistakes. Naturally, as you become more and more skilled, you will be able to accurately hit target areas closer and closer to the lines. On the other hand, being overly cautious by hitting every shot toward the center of your opponent's side of the court is also unwise. This tendency may be as dangerous as aiming at unrealistic targets such as the sidelines.

A critical factor in shot placement is watching the bird from racquet to racquet. This means focusing your eyes continually on the flight of the shuttle from the time it leaves your opponent's racquet until you actually hit it. At the same time, you must use your peripheral vision, to keep an eye on your opponent. An important part in the development of a player is learning how to concentrate on performing a skill while mentally processing other information. At first, you might not be able to perceive any details pertaining to your opponent while you are actually moving into position and hitting the bird. You may only note your opponent's initial court position or possibly some directional court movement. Eventually, as you gain experience, you will be able to know not only where your opponent is but also what will be his or her next move. This information will make your shot selection easier in both singles and doubles play.

Following are some guidelines regarding court areas you should aim to hit when obvious openings occur:

1. When an opponent is out of position, aim to the largest area of the court farthest away from the player. This is likely to be a safe shot because of the size of the target area.
2. When your opponent is moving, especially rapidly, hit the bird toward the area of the court just vacated. Hitting the shuttle behind your opponent is usually effective because to stop and change direction once momentum is built up is difficult. Also, to quickly change direction is taxing on a player's skill, strength, and endurance.
3. When your opponent is positioned in an ideal ready position and no apparent openings exist on the court, then hit or smash the bird directly at the racquet side of your opponent's body. This is more effective than a shot or smash to the court openings on either side because it crowds your opponent's return swing, resulting in a poor shot.
4. When playing doubles, a bird placed in the area of the court between your opponents can cause doubt as to who should hit it. This may result in no return, an error, or a poor return. (See Figure 8.1.)

The possible angles that the bird may travel in a return shot are other important factors that must be considered for successful shot performance. Angles are particularly critical in singles because one player must cover the entire court. When hitting a shot, try to place the shuttle in an area of the court that will narrow your opponent's angle of return. This will limit your opponent's possible return shots, thus increasing your chances to anticipate correctly. For example, if your serve is deep and near the center line, assuming a good ready stance at the base position places you approximately in the center of the angle of return and limits your opponent's choice of shots. However, if your serve is closer to the sideline, your opponent's options increase. The choice of a smash or a clear down the line is particularly effective and can be anticipated. Other possible shots that your opponent may execute from this position are a crosscourt slow drop or cut drop. These two shots are especially effective when the server is caught moving toward the open sideline to protect that area of the court.

This does not mean that you should never hit the bird toward the sidelines. However, you should be aware of the problems you might encounter if you hit the shuttle in that direction and your opponent has sufficient time to react and employ deception during the return shot. The same concept holds true for rallies as well as for serves. During a rally, logically you want to limit your opponent's time to rest, particularly on shots hit down the line when the angle of return is wider. Allowing your opponent less time to react between returns is a clear advantage of the attacking style of play. Attacking clears and shots directed downward are not as dangerous as defensive shots, even with a wide angle of return. These force your opponent to hit the bird up, giving you the advantage of time to get into position, apply deception, and hit an effective stroke.

The Changing Base

Where you position yourself on the court while waiting for a return will vary during the course of a contest. This position is dependent on several factors such as the type of shot you hit, the area of the court you hit it to, the skill level of your opponent, and your own ability to move and cover the court.

Generally speaking, a good base position to start from is the center of the court about five to six feet behind the short service line. (See Figure 8.2.) From this location, you can move effectively up, back, and from side to side to retrieve the bird. It is an excellent base position from which to reach the four corners of the court because moving forward is easier than moving backward. As previously mentioned, one's base position will vary during the course of a game, and players must adapt to meet specific needs by moving either closer to the net or deeper in the court. When determining your base position, you should consider the angle of return and the possible point of intercepting the shuttle. As you gain experience, this will become easier. You will learn to anticipate returns, and you will be able to adjust accordingly.

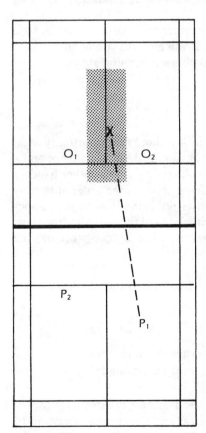

Figure 8.1 Hitting the bird between your opponents can cause doubt.

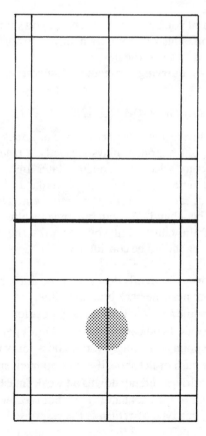

Figure 8.2 A good base position to start from is the center of the court.

When executing a shot, always try to hit the bird to an area of the court that will limit your opponent's choice of shots and possible angles of return. For instance, if you hit a clear to your opponent's backhand, *drift* a foot or two from your center base position to the same side of the court where you hit the shuttle. This enables you to reach the down-the-line return. On crosscourt shots, the shuttle must travel a farther distance, allowing you some additional time to reach it. In the same way, shots hit to your opponent's forehand side and deep in the court should trigger a slight drift to that side to protect against a quick return near that sideline.

During a series of clears, you should always be *fudging* slightly forward in anticipation of a drop shot. After playing a slow drop or a hairpin shot, do not return to base. Hold your position momentarily, and be ready to put away a weak return. If your opponent attempts to hit a clear, the angle necessary to get the bird over the net is such that it probably will not travel much past half court. When this occurs, you can easily slide back to a good position and smash it for a winner. Such *cheating* from the base position is just the opposite of the lazy or fatigued player's failure to return to base. Anticipation is the hallmark of a fit, experienced, and aggressive player and often yields great dividends for a relatively small investment of energy.

Until you become experienced, you should always try to return to the center court, or base position. This will not only help you to form good habits. It will also put you in an excellent position to await the next return. Otherwise, you will find yourself running about the court foolishly, hurrying to execute a desperate shot.

Defending Against the Smash

While the basic strategy is one of attack, you cannot attack without the opportunity to do so. If your opponent plays perfectly, a true attack cannot be mounted. With patience and a varied shot selection, sooner or later an opening or setup will appear. On the other hand, if you become impatient or simply make a bad shot first, defense becomes the order of the day for you, rather than for your opponent. The prime defensive shot is the clear to your opponent's backhand. You can buy time by alternating clears with drops to the opposite front corner of the court until you can take the offensive. However, when a smash occurs, the following should be considered:

1. Move to a slightly deeper base position on the court than usual unless the smash is coming from near the back boundary line.
2. Assume a well balanced ready position.
3. Stay alert and cool under fire. Don't panic.
4. Respond accordingly. (Sometimes, only reflexes will determine your response.)
5. Hit push or net shots if your opponent smashes from near the back boundary line.
6. Use drives and tap downs on weak smashes.
7. Clear to the backhand. This shot is often the one of choice. The main disadvantage for using this type of return is the response it will elicit. Generally, it allows your opponent to give you more of the same game and places you continually on the defensive until an error or winner occurs. While this may seem exciting at first, it really isn't too much fun.

When In Doubt

At times during play you will have little choice as to what to do. For example, situations may arise when you are handcuffed by a good shot or when you may just barely get to the bird. You might even be caught out of position or in some other precarious predicament in which little or no time for shot selection is available. Should this occur, the basic response is a high, deep defensive clear to your opponent's backhand. While this is no guarantee to get you off the hook, it will buy you some time and allow you to regain your base and composure.

Tactics In Serving

Strategies involving the service are simple and clear-cut. The serve, as an upward shot, is clearly defensive. The primary function of the serve is to prevent your opponent from gaining an overwhelming offensive advantage. Regardless of the type of serve you choose, precision and accuracy are absolutely necessary. Sloppy serving or poor execution can instill confidence in your opponent and make you lose the game.

Your serve should prevent smashes or other winning shots from being hit. However, it should always have sufficient force and accuracy to land in your opponent's receiving court. Nothing is more frustrating or demoralizing than to watch your unreturned serve land out-of-bounds. A mixture of serves will keep your opponent off balance and guessing. However, once you find a serve that works, keep serving it the entire game and match. Never change a winning serve. Only change one that is ineffective or one that your opponent has learned how to return effectively. Particularly in doubles play, you should change an ineffective serve or you will end up being both dominated and intimidated by a foe who can take advantage of your predictability.

After you execute the serve, move quickly to the base position. Always assume that your serve will be returned. If not, you will pay for your complacency by not being ready for the return. For additional information about serving, review Chapter 6.

Table 8.1   Guide To Serving

Game	Primary serve	Alternate serves
Singles	High, deep serve	Drive or low, short serves
Doubles	Low, short serve	Drive or flick serves

Note—The primary target areas for the serves are shown in Figures 6.4, 6.5, and 6.6.

Returning the Serve

As the receiver, always keep in mind that the serve is a defensive shot. According to the rules, it must be hit upward. This means that you should be able to make a good return. To serve an ace is very difficult. Should the server make a weak or poor serve, pounce on it immediately. Assume the offensive as soon as the shuttle passes over the net into your court. Do not let the server recover. Maintain your advantage and exploit any and all weaknesses.

While awaiting the serve in the right service court, assume the ready position about four to six feet from the short service line near the centerline if you are right-handed. Left-handed players should stand near the sideline. The reverse is true in the left service court. Left-handed players stand near the centerline while right-handed players take a position close to the sideline. These court positions are assumed to protect the often more vulnerable backhand. Of course, what constitutes the proper court position is variable. The area where you stand will depend on several factors such as reach, quickness, skill, and experience. The suggested receiving areas are good starting points and you can modify them according to your own abilities.

The majority of serves in singles will be high and deep. They are generally returned with a defensive clear. Occasionally, though, you should hit a drop shot to keep your opponent guessing. For serves that are not hit too deep, a smash is in order.

When a drive serve is executed, the return generally calls for a push or drive down the sideline. Low serves, on the other hand, are best returned by delaying contact with the bird as long as possible and then playing a tight net shot or a deceptive flick for an attacking clear to the backhand side, depending on your opponent's court position.

Remember that, regardless of where you position yourself to receive the serve, you alone are responsible for retrieving the shuttle. If you stand too far out of position to protect one aspect of your game or a particular area of the court, you make it easier for the server to aim for the area you have left unprotected.

Lastly, whatever shot you may use to return the serve is largely dependent on your skill and the type of serve employed. Learn to execute all of the various types of badminton shots; otherwise, you will be limited as to what you can do with the return.

Some Service Return Pointers
1. Assume a good ready stance while awaiting the serve.
2. Return high, short serves with an offensive shot.
3. Return high, deep serves with a defensive shot.
4. Vary the service return.
5. Keep your eye on the shuttle from service to return.
6. Select a position in the receiving court that will allow you to reach and return all of your opponent's serves.
7. Move quickly to the base position after returning the serve.
8. Watch your opponent with peripheral vision so you know what type of return to execute.
9. Play the percentages, and choose a safe return when you are behind or the game is close.

Doubles Strategy

Play is much faster in doubles because more shots are being hit. Also, shots have to be more accurate because there is less open area of the court. However, doubles is physically less demanding than singles. Both partners have a smaller area of the court to cover.

The psychology for doubles play is somewhat different than for singles. In doubles, you have to rely on your partner. Both players must avoid costly errors, serve and return shots accurately, and work harmoniously on the court. Teamwork is essential for a winning combination.

Selecting a Partner

Before playing doubles, especially in tournament competition, find a partner with compatible skills, temperament, and style of play. Finding a player with whom you can work and communicate is very important.

Right handed players should look for and team up with left handed players and vice versa. A righty-lefty team is ideal because the majority of shots can be forehand strokes. If you are unable to pair up with a righty or lefty, whichever is the case, then look for someone who can compensate for your weaknesses. Prior to searching for a partner, analyze your skills. A correct assessment of your own strengths and weaknesses will help you to choose a partner who can complement your skills. Being able to recognize the strengths and weaknesses of potential partners also helps in the development of a successful doubles team. Once you select a partner, the next step is to practice and play together often. Follow these practice sessions with regular discussions of strategy. Combining these factors will help you to become a more cohesive unit and to achieve better play and court coverage.

Serving in Doubles

Serving is an extremely important aspect of successful doubles play. The primary key is accuracy. A poor serve is often returned for an outright winner. Before serving, let your partner know the type and the direction of the serve you intend to execute. This provides your team with a slight advantage because you know where the bird will travel. This knowledge permits both partners on the serving team to move quickly to a good defensive position on the court to await the return.

As soon as the bird is served, players (especially the server) should move quickly to the correct court position. The nonserving partner of the team assumes the correct court position either prior to the serve or as the shuttle is served. Where each person stands will depend on the type of doubles formation the team employs. (See Figure 8.3.)

The low serve is the primary serve used in doubles competition. It is very effective when used in combination with the flick and drive serves. Once again, the type of serve you use will be dictated by your own abilities and the skill levels of the individuals you are playing against. Prior to a match, scout your opponents to learn which serve might be effective. Then, practice it.

Figure 8.3 *Serving in doubles. The nonserving partner assumes a position in center court near the rear service line.*

Receiving in Doubles

The receiving position in doubles is approximately one to three feet behind the short service line near the centerline or sideline, depending on which court you are receiving in. The foot opposite the racquet hand is forward. Your weight is over the balls of your feet. You raise the racquet high above your head, threatening mayhem on any weak service! The diagonal stance allows quick movement forward and backward, so necessary in retrieving the various flights of the shuttle. Many excellent players prefer the *frying pan grip* for this situation.

The receiver's partner is stationed somewhat deeper, close to the centerline, but not so close as to interfere with play of the serve. This position allows a natural flow pattern for assumption of either the *up-and-back* or the *side-by-side formation,* depending on how the service is returned.

Most serves are usually hit low and toward the centerline. As the receiver, you should attempt to hit the shuttle as early as possible after it crosses the net. Use a sharp downward tap, a drive or push down the sideline, or a straight drop. Avoid crosscourt returns. Drive serves are usually best handled by push shots, while high serves or flicks should be smashed. The effectiveness of your service return will determine whether or not your team can either score an outright winner or be aggressive and take the initiative. A poor or ineffective return will result in a setup and will immediately place your team back on the defensive. Although any of the badminton shots can be used to return the serve in doubles competition, the crucial point is to hit the right one at the right time. Try not to hit a service return that will compromise your team's position. When possible, try for a winner. Otherwise, try to return the shuttle to the weaker player of the opposing team. This will increase the percentages for a mistake or a poor return.

Choosing a Doubles Formation

The strategy and tactics a doubles team will use during a contest is largely determined by the system of formation that they employ. Two basic formations are used in badminton, the side-by-side and the up-and-back formations. No matter which system you use, the essential ingredient for success is teamwork.

Side-by-Side Formation.   The side-by-side system of doubles play is the one most frequently used by beginners because the responsibilities of each player are clearly defined and they allow for the development of all-around skills. In this system of play, the court is divided into two equal parts from the net to the end line. Partners are responsible for all shuttles hit to their particular side of the court. If both players are either right- or left-handed, the player who has the better forehand shot has the responsibility for all shuttles hit to the center of the court. When one player is right-handed and the other left-handed, then prior to play the partners must decide who will take the shots down the center.

The side-by-side formation is particularly well suited for defensive play but does not lend itself to attack. It provides your opponent the opportunity to pick on the weaker player. (See Figure 8.4.)

Up-and-Back Formation.   Sometimes called the *front-and-back* or *I formation,* the up-and back is a strong attacking system of play and makes it easy to take advantage of differences in ability and strength. For instance, a weaker player can be more effective in the *up* position close to the net. The up player's responsibility is to play all net shots and to intercept pushes and drives down the sideline whenever possible. The base position for this player is the center of the court on the short service line. Since the player is so close to the net and to the op-

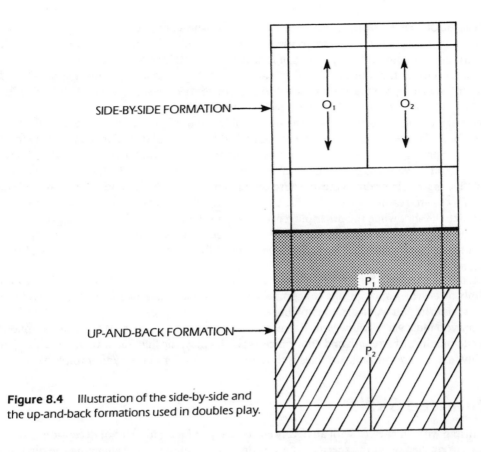

SIDE-BY-SIDE FORMATION

UP-AND-BACK FORMATION

Figure 8.4 Illustration of the side-by-side and the up-and-back formations used in doubles play.

ponents, the choked frying pan grip is used. This allows the quicker movement of the racquet necessary in this vulnerable position.

The *back* player in this formation uses the standard grip and is responsible for all shuttles hit in the deep court and those that pass the up player. This player's base position is on the centerline, about six feet behind the partner. Good target areas to aim for when playing against this formation are midcourt on the sides, the box at the back player's backhand, and directly at the racquet side (shoulder to hip) of either opponent. Crosscourt smashes should be avoided. Generally, they are not effective in doubles, unless both opponents are caught out of position and to one side of the court. Doubles play lends itself more to the *power game* than to defensive play. Smashes are more frequent than in singles. Another difference in shot selection is that few slow drops are used in doubles; the defensive up player will make this shot ineffective.

During mixed doubles, the woman nearly always plays the up position. Although she has a smaller area of the court to cover, hers is a critical assignment, requiring quick reflexes and good judgment. In order to be able to assume the up-and-back configuration when the man is serving, the woman stations herself on the short service line and to his left, if he is right-handed, regardless of which court he is serving to. The man, in turn, has to make an adjustment by serving from a deeper position so that he can assume the back position quickly. With a woman who is a strong player, a team might prefer that the man serve from the normal position near the junction of the short service line and the centerline.

Combination, or Rotation, Formation.   Those who combine the side-by-side and up-and-back formations achieve perhaps the strongest team play. For women's or men's doubles competition, the combination formation is clearly the superior system of play. In this procedure, when hitting the shuttle upward to your opponents, assume the defensive side-by-side positions. When the shuttle is hit upward to your team, take the attacking, or offensive, up-and-back position of play. These two rules are simple and easy to follow. Deciding who goes where when changing formations is the only problem that might occur. Movement from the up-and-back formation to side-by-side is controlled by the up player. The back player simply takes his or her cue from the up player's movement and fills the void in the vacant slot. The up player should move to the side away from the shuttle, allowing the back player to respond to a smash that is straight or down the line. Crosscourt smashes are slower and can be handled well enough by the retreating player. To shift back when a lifted bird appears, the player closest to it will take the shot while the other player moves to protect the net area. An exception occurs when the shot is taken from midcourt or closer. Since the player hitting the smashes is only a step or two away from the up player's base position, this player remains up, with the partner assuming the back position.

Rotating from one formation to another may sound somewhat complex, but it need not be. Only a few rules and options concerning movement pattern are necessary. By playing together regularly, you will learn the flowing action characteristic of winning teams. For this to happen, you must get to know your partner's play as well as your own. While doubles play is not as demanding of strength and endurance as singles play, the fluid teamwork is exciting, incredibly fast, and rewarding. Doubles is the game of choice for many badminton fans.

Advanced Skills

Hitting with an open or with an overly closed racquet face adds a bit of deception. The resulting cut or slice slows the speed of the shuttle while simultaneously changing the direction of the flight. An effective application of this stroke can be made on returning clears or serves near the sideline. With exactly the same motion as a smash down the line to your opponent, the open face and a tiny change in racquet path (swing) can send a crosscourt cut drop that is extremely tough to handle. Cuts or slices are also very effective in net play. Two prerequisites for these shots are (1) enough time to make the necessary adjustments and (2) a high level of skill.

Holding the shuttle might sound illegal, but it is actually an advanced skill employed mostly on returns of drop shots. The stroke begins with a cocked wrist. If the opponent rushes the net, a little flick of the wrist for an attacking clear usually becomes a winner. If your opponent stays at the base or commits backward, the wrist stays cocked and results in a tight net or hairpin shot. Again, the keys to success are plenty of time and mastery of the skill.

Double-motion strokes also require lots of time, advanced skill, and natural athletic ability. Faking in one direction and hitting in another, the double-motion shot, is extremely demanding and should be undertaken only when you are comfortable with the demands of ordinary strokes.

All of these advanced techniques should be practiced, analyzed, and practiced again before implementing them in competition. Chapter 10 provides additional drills to help you polish up these skills and to evaluate your readiness to use them.

9
Skill Performance Activities

This chapter contains a progression of practical experiences for players who are serious about learning the game of badminton. These activities will help lay the proper groundwork for mastery of basic skills and techniques prior to competition. If you follow this systematic approach, your skills will become much better and your playing enhanced.

Begin this set of activities only after you have read the corresponding skill descriptions in the text or your instructor has presented the skill. Having both an intellectual understanding of the task and proper instructions will allow better analysis of your play and quicker mastery of the techniques.

The tasks have been designed from the simple to the more complex. Some, presented near the end of this chapter, can be handled only by fairly skilled and athletic individuals. Most individuals can learn them by the end of a one-semester class or perhaps in an intermediate-level class. Keep in mind that badminton is an absurdly easy game to learn, but an immensely difficult game to master. If some of the assignments presented here seem especially difficult to perform, do not be discouraged. Be tenacious, but be realistic as well.

Assignment 1: Forehand Grip

Working with a partner, discuss the elements of the proper forehand grip (see Chapter 5). Practice holding the racquet with the forehand grip, critiquing each other. When you feel confident that you can correctly hold the racquet for a forehand shot, close your eyes and assume the proper grip ten times in a row. Each time, your partner should evaluate your performance.

Check Points

1. Is your grip similar to a handshake?
2. Is the racquet face perpendicular to the floor, and is a *V* formed by your thumb and forefinger on the top level of the handle, pointing to your racquet-hand shoulder?
3. Is the forefinger on the bottom of the racquet handle when the racquet face is perpendicular to the floor?
4. Is the forefinger spread slightly away from the other fingers?
5. Is the grip gentle?

Evaluation.   If you can answer yes to each question at least seven out of ten times, then move on to the next technique.

Assignment 2: Backhand Grip

Working with your partner, discuss and practice the backhand grip. Critique each other as you change your grip from the forehand to the backhand. When you feel that you can grip the racquet correctly, then try it ten times with your eyes closed. Have your partner critique your performance, and answer these questions:

Check Points

1. Is the change of grip smooth and easy?
2. Is the thumb squarely on the back bevel?
3. Is the knuckle of the forefinger now on top of the racquet handle when the racquet face is perpendicular to the floor?
4. Is the forefinger closer to the other fingers than it was in the forehand grip?
5. Is the grip gentle?

Evaluation.   If you can answer yes to each question at least seven out of ten times, move on to the next assignment.

Assignment 3: Ready Position

Initially, discuss the elements of the proper ready position with your partner. Take turns moving into this stance, starting from a relaxed position. Once you both feel comfortable with the task, attempt this movement ten times. Each time, have your partner critique your performance.

Check Points

1. Are you facing the net with your head up?
2. Are your knees and hips slightly flexed?
3. Is your weight on the balls of your feet?
4. Are the feet about shoulder width apart?
5. Is the racquet held about chest level with the forehand grip, and is the other (nonracquet) hand touching the neck of the racquet?

Evaluation.   Before moving to the next step, you should be able to answer yes to each question at least seven out of ten times.

Assignment 4: Short Serve Using the Forehand Stroke

First, discuss the proper short serve technique with your partner. Next, hit short serves to each other at least ten times, critiquing each other's mechanics. Ignore the results (i.e., where the bird lands) at this time. Once you learn the proper mechanics, make ten short serves to your partner, who will let the birds fall and record the results.

Check Points

1. Is the serving stance correct (about three feet from the front service line, nonracquet foot slightly advanced toward the net)?

2. Is the wrist cocked prior to each serve?

3. Is there a weight transfer from back to front foot during the swing?

4. Is contact made with the bird below waist height?

Evaluation.   Proceed to the next assignment only when you can answer yes to each question at least eight of ten times and all serves land in the proper court.

Assignment 5: Forehand Short Serve to a Target

Review with your partner the elements of the short serve. Place a rope parallel to and twenty inches above the net. Serve ten birds for practice, aiming at targets in the service court. (See Figures 9.1 and 9.2 for scoring.) Use either service scoring system to check your accuracy.

Check Points

1. Is the stance comfortable, with the body erect?

2. Is there little or no uncocking of the wrist?

3. Is the action more of a guiding or pushing than a hit?

4. Is the racquet follow-through smooth, and does it follow a line toward the target until it is about waist high?

5. Do all shots pass through the gap between the net and the suspended rope?

Evaluation.   No points are allowed for shuttles that pass over the rope. One bonus point is scored for each shuttle that passes between the rope and the net. Double points are given for those that touch the net and land on the target. Use the scoring chart in Appendix B to record your scores. After you score a minimum of 30 points, move to the next technique.

Assignment 6: Short Serve Using the Backhand Stroke

Discuss the mechanics of this stroke with your partner. Review the basic differences, similarities, advantages, and disadvantages of the backhand and the forehand short serves. Then, hit several short serves (minimum ten) to each other, disregarding results. Each time, critique your partner's stroke technique. Follow this with ten more short serves to your partner, who will allow the birds to fall into the receiving zone. Record the results, and evaluate your performance.

Check Points

1. Is the grip slightly shortened?

2. Is the shuttle held just above the waist and well out in front of the body?

3. Is the elbow of the racquet arm held high?

4. Is the wrist kept cocked throughout, resulting in more of a push than a hit?

5. Is the bird contacted clearly below the waist?

Evaluation.   Only when your partner answers yes to each question eight out of ten times and all serves land in the proper court should you proceed to the next assignment.

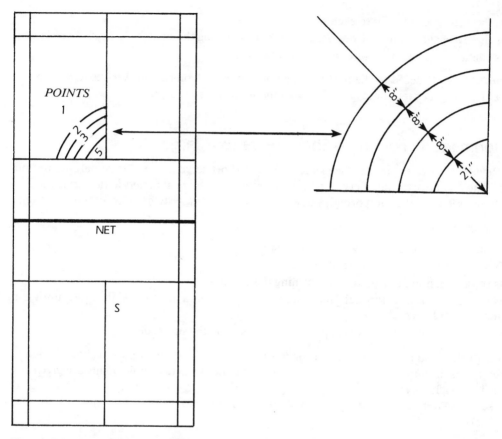

Figure 9.1 Scoring target areas for the short serve. (Adapted from a test by Scott and French.)

Assignment 7: Backhand Short Serve to a Target

Using the same target area and procedure described in Assignment 5, hit at least ten birds to the target for practice before serving for a score.

Check Points

1. Is the stance comfortable and the body erect?
2. Is there little or no uncocking of the wrist?
3. Is the action more of a guiding or pushing than a hit?
4. Is the grip shortened and the elbow of the racquet arm held high?
5. Did all shots go between the net and the rope?

Evaluation.   No points are scored for shuttles that pass over the rope. One bonus point is awarded for each shuttle passing between the rope and the net. Double points are awarded for those touching the net and landing on the target. Record scores on the log sheets provided in Appendix B. When you can score at least 30 points, move on to another task.

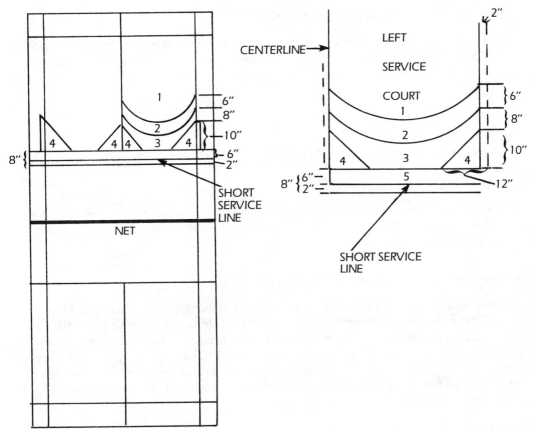

Figure 9.2 Alternate scoring target areas for short serve.

Assignment 8: Long Serve

Discuss the elements of the long serve with your partner. Pay close attention to the differences, similarities, and methods of deception (i.e., ways of disguising the serve until the last moment). Hit long serves to one another at least ten times, paying more attention to technique than to where the bird lands. Critique each other's serving mechanics. Once proper technique is learned, try to hit the birds to the proper area.

Check Points

1. Is the action very similar to that of the forehand short serve until just before contact?
2. Does a strong uncocking of the wrist generate power?
3. Does hip and shoulder rotation precede the wrist action?
4. Is there a clear follow-through toward the shoulder of the nonracquet arm?
5. Is the trajectory very high and deep, with the bird dropping almost vertically near the back line?

Evaluation. When you can answer yes to each question eight out of ten times and make at least eight serves land in the proper court, go on to the next task.

Assignment 9: Long Serve to a Target

Review the elements of the long serve with your partner. Hit ten warm-up serves at the target (see Figure 9.3 for dimensions). Each serve should pass over your partner's racquet, extended overhead. Hit ten long serves, and record the score.

Check Points

1. Is plenty of power generated?
2. Do all serves pass over the rope?
3. Are serves hit high enough? (If not, they will be too long.)
4. Are resulting shots fairly consistent?
5. Is the follow-through strong and high?

Evaluation.   No points are awarded for birds that touch or pass lower than your partner's racquet. Before proceeding to Assignment 10, you should attain a score of 30 points or better. Record scores on data sheets provided in Appendix C.

Assignment 10: Forehand Overhead Clear

Go over with your partner the procedures for successfully completing the overhead clear shot. Review the similarities among this shot, an overhand throw, and a tennis serve. Hit ten successive clears back and forth, concentrating on proper mechanics. Then, have your partner hit ten long serves just short of the long service line for doubles. Return each with a clear. After serving, your partner should ignore the flight of the bird and concentrate on watching how well you execute the fundamentals of the clear. After each shot, have your partner critique your performance.

Check Points

1. As the bird comes toward you, do you point at it with the nonracquet arm? (This movement encourages shoulder rotation, which produces more power when the shot is made.)
2. Is the weight initially on the back foot?
3. Is the racquet held in a back-scratching position in preparation for the shot?
4. Is the shot very similar to throwing the racquet?
5. Is the bird contacted at the highest possible point?

Evaluation.   When you can answer yes to each of the questions eight out of ten times and your returns land in the court, move on to the assignment on clearing to a target.

Assignment 11: Forehand Overhead Clear to a Target

Set up the target, and follow the same procedure outlined in Assignment 10. Review the techniques for hitting an overhead clear shot. Next, have your partner hit long serves that land just short of the long service line for doubles. Move from the base position to make each return. After several warm-up clears have been hit, make ten forehand overhead clears and record the results.

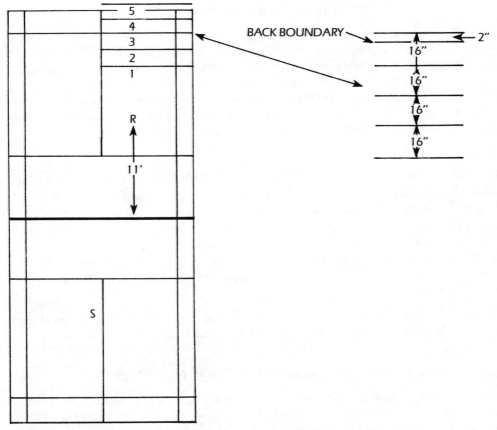

Figure 9.3 Scoring target areas for the long serve (adapted from a test by Poole).

Check Points

1. Is contact made almost directly overhead, perhaps slightly in front of the body because of the backward lean prior to the shot?
2. Is there strong hip and shoulder rotation?
3. Does your body weight shift from the back to the front foot?
4. Is the shuttle hit with a flat face? (This requires wrist rotation inward during the wrist flexion, or snap.)
5. Do the racquet and hand make almost a ninety-degree angle with the arm at the end of the follow-through?

Evaluation.   After answering yes to each question eight out of ten times and making a total score of 30 points or higher, proceed to the backhand clear assignments. Record your score on the log sheets provided in Appendix D.

Assignment 12: Backhand Overhead Clear

Carefully review materials and methods of the backhand grip and the basic backhand overhead stroke. Know and understand why it is even more important to hit the bird as high as possible with the backhand as it is with the forehand, particularly on the clear. Begin practice by hitting at least ten successive clears back and forth with your partner while concentrating on the proper mechanics. Then, have your partner hit ten long serves just short of the long service line for doubles and return each with a backhand clear. Your partner should let the birds fall, ignoring the result and concentrating on evaluating your stroke.

Check Points

1. Do you rotate your trunk so that your chest approximately faces the left rear corner of the court when moving into position to execute the shot?
2. Is there strong trunk rotation toward the net during the shot?
3. Does the elbow of the racquet arm point at the bird just prior to initiating the forward action of the stroke?
4. Are the racquet and forearm pointed down toward the floor as the shuttle approaches?
5. Is the action sequence: hip rotation, trunk rotation, upper arm movement, forearm movement, wrist snap?

Evaluation. When you can answer yes to each question eight out of ten times and at least eight land in the proper court, record the result in Assignment 13.

Assignment 13: Backhand Overhead Clear to a Target

Carefully review again the requirements for properly making this stroke. This is one of the most difficult shots to execute, unless the skill becomes a truly coordinated action. Otherwise, few players are strong enough to clear the shuttle from deep in their court to the baseline in the opponent's court. You must clearly understand the elements of the shot before you can perform it well. After attempting ten practice clears, have your partner set you up with ten long serves that will land just short of the long service line for doubles. Return each shot to the target area illustrated in Figure 9.3. Make sure the shuttle clears the rope each time. (This is the same setup that was used for Assignment 9.) The bird must be allowed to fall so your partner can score your performance.

Check Points

1. Is the shuttle contact at the highest point possible?
2. Is the shuttle contacted slightly in front of the body?
3. Is powerful wrist action employed?
4. Is the follow-through upward and forward?
5. Is a clear weight shift from the back to the front foot evident during the shot?

Evaluation. When you can answer these points affirmatively eight out of ten times and your score is 25 or above, move to the next assignment. Record your results on the data sheet provided in Appendix D.

Assignment 14: Forehand Smash

Discuss the elements of the smash, including differences and similarities when compared to: (1) an overhand throw, (2) a tennis serve, and (3) a badminton clear. Practice the motion at least ten times, without a shuttle. Critique one another carefully. Then, have your partner hit ten high serves to you at each of the following locations: (1) junction of the centerline and the short service line, (2) in the center of the court about halfway between the short service line and the long service line for doubles, and (3) in center court just short of the long service line for doubles. Smash each serve, noting the differences in results as you move away from the net.

Check Points

1. Is the bird contacted well in front of the body?
2. Is the flight of the shuttle distinctly downward?
3. Is the shuttle contacted at the highest possible point?
4. Does the nonracquet arm point at the bird on its downward flight, ensuring good rotation?
5. Does the racquet move from the back-scratching position with a powerful arm action, followed by a strong wrist snap?

Evaluation.   When you can answer each question yes an average of eight out of ten shots, and can execute 100 percent of the smashes from the closest position, 80 percent from the middle court position, and 60 percent from the deepest area in the court, move on to practice hitting the smash to a target.

Assignment 15: Forehand Smash to a Target

Review the procedures that led to your success in Assignment 14. What aspects of the smash gave you the most trouble? Smashing to a target combines the skills covered in the previous assignment with a need for accuracy. Place three hula-hoops on the court about halfway between the short service line and the long service line for doubles. One should be over the centerline and the other two should just touch the sidelines for singles. (See Figure 9.4.) Following ten warm-up smashes, have your partner hit five high serves to you at the junction of the centerline and the short service line, followed by five more to you in center court. Immediately after hitting the shuttle, have your partner call, "Right," "Left," or "Center." Upon hearing the call, try to adjust your position and stroke to smash the shuttle toward the appropriate hoop.

Check Points

1. Is the shuttle hit with a racquet face that is square to the shuttle's flight? (Some attention should be given to inward rotation of the wrist during the snap if the answer is no.)
2. Is the shuttle contacted twelve to eighteen inches in front of the body?
3. Is the whole arm snapped straight at impact?
4. Does the racquet head accelerate smoothly, starting with the backswing and continuing through impact?
5. Is the footwork effective in moving you into position to hit the shuttle to each of the target areas?

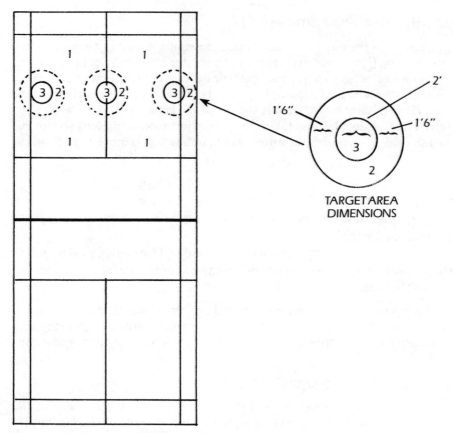

Figure 9.4   Scoring target areas for smashes.

Evaluation.   Score 3 points for each smash that hits the correct target, 2 points for each shuttle that lands within the outer circle of the target, and 1 point for smashes that simply land in the court. When you answer yes to each of the questions for four out of five shots at each position and your total score for the ten shots is 20 points or better, move on. Record scores on the smash shot log sheet in Appendix E.

Assignment 16: Around-the-Head Smash

This shot is often preferred by many players over the backhand smash. The around-the-head smash is an advanced stroke. Before attempting it, review the mechanics of the stroke with your partner. Volley a minimum of ten shots as a preliminary warm up. Then, have your partner hit ten long serves slightly to your backhand side, five as you stand on the short service line, and five as you are stationed in midcourt. Use an around-the-head smash to return each shot.

Check Points

1. Is the shuttle above or beyond the shoulder of the nonracquet hand?
2. Is the body square to the net and arched sideways over the nonracquet foot?
3. Is your body weight solidly over the nonracquet foot?
4. Does the forearm of the racquet arm pass over the top of the head?
5. Is there good wrist snap, despite the unnatural position?

Evaluation. If the answer to four out of five questions is yes for each court position and eight of the ten smashes are reasonably powerful and hit into your opponent's side of the court, go to the next assignment.

Assignment 17: Drives

Discuss how to hit a drive shot with your partner. Next, have your partner hit serves that you cannot smash, but that you can hit before they drop below the tape. Try to play the shots from midcourt. First, hit ten returns from your forehand side and then ten from the backhand. On the ones to your backhand, play either an around-the-head drive or a backhand drive. The type of return shot will depend primarily on how close the path of the shuttle is to your body.

Check Points

1. Is the return trajectory of the shuttle such that it almost skims the net and is directed flatly or slightly down?
2. Is the action for forehand drives similar to throwing the racquet sidearm at the shuttle?
3. Does the elbow lead on backhand drives by pointing at the oncoming shuttle?
4. Are you flexible and agile enough to hit an around-the-head drive on a low shuttle? (If not, stick to the backhand drive when a drive from the off side is called for.)
5. Is there a flat follow-through for all drives?

Evaluation. When the answers to questions 1 through 3 and 5 are yes for eight out of ten shots for both forehands and backhands and eight of the ten land in the court, then proceed to the next task.

Assignment 18: Drives to a Target

Review the mechanics of the forehand and backhand drives, going through the motions of the shots without a shuttle. The primary areas to aim for are the alleys down either sideline. Have your partner hit shots to you about net height. Return each with a drive shot. After taking ten practice shots, hit ten for a score. Shuttles landing in the alley count 3 points, and those within three feet of the alley and in the court count 1 point. (See Figure 9.5.)

Check Points

1. Is the proper grip used for both strokes?
2. Is the stance correct?

3. Does the racquet head on forehand shots accelerate from almost touching the back in a flat arc through the wrist snap?

4. Is the racquet hand for the backhand almost touching the opposite shoulder with the racquet elbow aimed at the oncoming shuttle as the stroke commences?

5. Is the action for backhand and forehand explosive?

Evaluation.   After answering yes eight out of ten times to each question for both forehand and backhand shots and having scored on each side at least 28 points, go on to the next task. Record your score on the drive shot log sheets in Appendix F.

Assignment 19: Overhand Forehand Drop Shot

After you and your partner critique the mechanics of the drop shot, practice ten swings without birds. Next, have your partner hit ten long serves to your forehand court, so you can execute drop shot returns.

Check Points

1. Is the action exactly like a clear up to the point of contact?

2. Is good body rotation performed?

3. Is the wrist cocked and the racquet in the back-scratch position as the stroke begins?

4. Does body weight shift forward with the stroke?

5. Do you slow the racquet head speed upon contact?

Evaluation.   If you disguise your shots well, all questions are answered yes on eight of the ten shots, and eight of ten fall between the net and the short service line (double credit for those touching the net and falling short), proceed to Assignment 20. A minimum score of 24 points is needed before moving on. Record scores on the drop shot log sheet in Appendix G. (See Figure 9.6.)

Assignment 20: Overhead Backhand Drop Shot

Review the drop shot verbally with your partner, and then make ten strokes without a bird. Have your stroke critiqued after each shot. Let your partner hit ten high serves to your backhand court. Return each with a drop shot.

Check Points

1. Is this stroke exactly like the overhead backhand clear until the moment of contact?

2. Is the bird contacted as high as possible?

3. Do you perform good trunk rotation and weight shift?

4. Is the follow-through like that of the smash, except slower?

5. Is acceleration of the racquet slowed just prior to contact?

Evaluation.   Shots falling between the net and the short service line are scored 3 points; those touching the net and falling in this area are scored double. When you can score at least 20 points and answer yes eight out of ten times to the questions, go to the next assignment. Record scores in Appendix G.

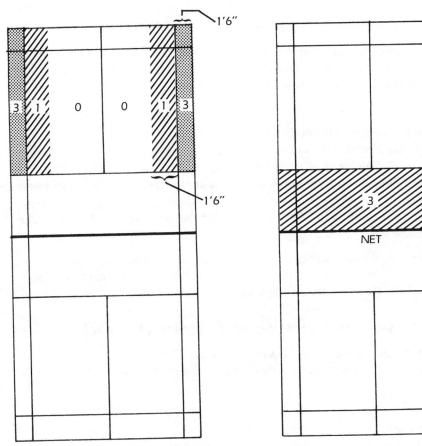

Figure 9.5 Scoring target areas for drives.   **Figure 9.6** Scoring target area for drop shots.

Assignment 21: Backhand Smash

This is a most difficult shot, but logically should follow mastery of the backhand clear and the backhand drop. Compare the mechanics of these three shots. How are they similar? What are the basic differences? Imitate the backhand smash without using a bird. After ten trials, all critiqued by your partner, return ten long serves hit to your backhand side. Five should be hit to you at the short service line and five at midcourt. Smash each.

Check Points
1. Does the elbow point toward the oncoming shuttle, and is the racquet pointing downward at the backswing, prior to initiating the power generation by the legs and trunk?
2. Is weight shifted from back to front foot, along with good hip and trunk rotation?
3. Is the shuttle contacted as high as possible?
4. Is the wrist snap timed to give maximum power?
5. Is the power generated sufficient to be effective?

Evaluation.   When the answers to each question are yes for eight out of ten smashes and eight of the ten shots land in the court, move on to the next assignment.

Assignment 22: Forehand Short Serve, Intermediate Level

Review the short serve with your partner. Refer to Assignment 5 and Figure 9.1 for details as to how to set up the target and test. The only difference is that the rope is now strung only twelve inches over the net. Following a series of ten practice serves, serve ten for score.

Check Points

1. Is the stance comfortable, with the body erect?
2. Does the wrist remain almost fully cocked?
3. Is the action more of a guiding or pushing action than a hit?
4. Does the racquet follow through smoothly on line toward the target until it is about waist high?
5. Do all shots pass through the gap between the net and the rope suspended twelve inches above?

Evaluation.   No points are allowed for shuttles that pass over the rope. Double points are given for those that touch the net and land on the target area. When you can score 30 points or more, go to the next task. Record scores in Appendix B.

Assignment 23: Backhand Short Serve, Intermediate Level

The same setup (target and rope) is used as in Assignment 22. Go through the elements of this serve with your partner, critiquing each other's practice serves (ten each). Then, serve ten for scoring.

Check Points

1. Is the grip shortened?
2. Is the shuttle held by the skirt, just above the waist and well out in front of the body?
3. Is the elbow of the racquet arm held high?
4. Is the wrist kept cocked throughout, resulting in more of a push than a hit?
5. Is the bird contacted clearly below the waist?

Evaluation.   No points are given for birds that travel over the rope, but double points are given for those that touch the net and land on the target. When you can answer yes to each question eight out of ten times, and you score at least 30 points, move on. Record the scores in Appendix B.

Assignment 24: Forehand Flick Serve

Review, with your partner, the fundamentals of the flick serve. In what circumstances is it best used? What are the relative advantages and disadvantages? Serve ten to each other, ignoring the outcome, but rather critiquing the mechanics of each stroke. Then, serve ten more for score, letting each fall. Your partner should critique your execution of each shot.

Check Points

1. Does the serve look exactly like the low, short serve until just prior to the racquet contacting the shuttle?

2. Does a sharp wrist action *flick* the shuttle over the reach of your opponent?
3. Is the swing the same length as for the low short serve?
4. Is the swing the same speed as for the low short serve?
5. Is the serve made without a preliminary look at the target?

Evaluation.   Accuracy on this task is judged by use of a target. (See Figure 9.3.) When the answer to the questions is yes for eight of ten serves and you score at least 20 points, you have successfully completed this task. Record the scores in Appendix H.

Assignment 25: Backhand Flick Serve

You and your partner should review carefully the mechanics of making the backhand flick serve. Concentrate on similarities with the low, short backhand serve; deception is the key to success for this stroke. What are the basic differences between the two serves? Using the same procedures as in Assignment 24, make ten serves for score after a preliminary warm up. You and your partner should critique one another's warm ups and serves for score.

Check Points

1. Is the stroke exactly like the low short serve up to the moment of impact?
2. Are length and speed of stroke identical to those for the low short serve?
3. Is the wrist snap strong enough to clear the outstretched racquet of your partner?
4. Is the bird held well out in front of the body and exactly between your body and that of the receiver?
5. Did you look at the target prior to the serve?

Evaluation.   When the answer to each question is yes for eight out of ten shots and the score is at least 20 points by the criteria set up in Figure 9.3, go on to another task. Record the scores in Appendix H.

Assignment 26: Forehand Drive Serve

Discuss the components and strategic use of the drive serve with your partner. What are advantages and disadvantages to use of this serve from a stance near the sideline? Hit and critique ten drives to each other. Then, serve ten times for score, aiming at quarter-circle targets placed at the junction of the centerline and the long service line for doubles. (See Figure 9.7.)

Check Points

1. Is the trajectory fairly flat and the speed fast?
2. Is the shuttle contacted clearly below the waist? (The tendency with this shot is to fault by contacting the bird illegally high.)
3. Is the shot deceptive, looking like the short low serve until just before contact?
4. Do you give away the shot by visual targeting just before contact?
5. Is good wrist action employed, accomplishing the desired deception?

Evaluation.   When the answer is yes to the question on eight of ten serves and the total score is 20 points or better, move on. Record the scores in Appendix I.

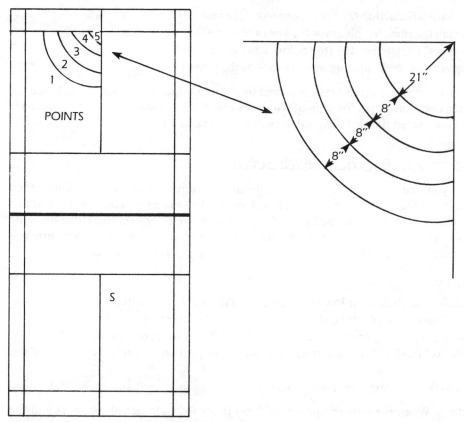

Figure 9.7 Scoring target area for drive serves.

Assignment 27: Backhand Drive Serve

Discuss the elements and strategy of the backhand drive serve. You and your partner should hit ten practice serves to each other, critiquing the mechanics. Then, hit ten for score, using the same target setup described in the preceding assignment on the forehand drive serve.

Check Points

1. Is the serve exactly like the low short serve and the flick serve until just prior to contacting the bird?

2. Did the server peek at the target?

3. Did the server use strong wrist snap?

4. Is this a flat, fast serve?

5. Is the action clearly within the rules of play?

Evaluation. When you answer yes eight out of ten times to each question and can score 20 points or better, proceed to the next task. Record the scores in Appendix I.

Assignment 28: Low Forehand Short Serve, Advanced Level

Review the low short serve and the procedures for Assignment 5. The only difference will be the height of the rope over the net; it should be set at six inches above the tape for this task. Following ten practice serves and critiques for each other's mechanics, make ten serves for

Check Points

1. Is the stance comfortable with the body erect?
2. Is the wrist uncocked?
3. Is the action more of a push than a strike?
4. Is the follow-through on line with the target until the racquet is about waist high?
5. Do all shuttles pass over the net and under the rope?

Evaluation. No points are awarded for serves that go over the rope. Double points are given for those that touch the net and land on target. A minimum of 30 points signifies adequate mastery of this assignment. Record scores in Appendix B.

Assignment 29: Low Backhand Short Serve, Advanced Level

Discuss the low short backhand serve with your partner. Follow the procedures for Assignment 28. Serve and critique ten shots for each other before serving ten times for score.

Check Points

1. Is the grip slightly shortened?
2. Is the shuttle held just above waist level and well out in front of the body?
3. Is the elbow of the racquet arm held high?
4. Is contact with the bird clearly below the waist?

Evaluation. When you answer yes to the questions eight out of ten tries and you can score 30 points or better, you have mastered this advanced technique. Remember, for scoring no points are given for shots over the rope, and double points accrue for those that touch the net and fall on the target. Record scores in Appendix B.

Summary

You should always strive to achieve excellence. Even after you have completed the first 29 assignments successfully, you should periodically return to this section for reevaluation. Frequent analysis of your play will help you to understand your current skill level and will recommend drills for fine tuning a particular shot or stroke. On your next time around, whichever tasks you should choose to repeat, set standards higher. This is easily done, simply by adjusting the evaluation procedures. Smaller targets or higher criterion scores or both will help you hone your skills to a sharp edge. Be as aggressive and creative in your planning for practice as you are in the game itself.

10
Advanced Badminton Drills

Drills serve a dual purpose. They sharpen your skill while simultaneously contributing to improving your fitness. The drills presented in this section are intermediate and advanced activities, which should be tackled after the skill performance tasks in Chapter 9. These require more continuous movement and can provide additional help toward simultaneous skill and conditioning development. To skip Chapter 9 in search of quick and easy progress would be a mistake. Only frustration will result when the basic strokes are not developed as a foundation.

In summary, be patient. For best results, work progressively to master the easier skills to an acceptable level, performing each basic drill before moving to more complex ones. Your instructor can guide you if you have problems. At all times, try to practice the proper grip, stance, and stroke mechanics. Through correct fundamentals and rigorous drill work, application of strategy becomes a simple matter and your success at badminton becomes more likely. How quickly you improve depends on the amount and quality of work and time you spend practicing your skills. The results you acheive will be proportionate to the effort you put into your practice sessions. Remember, hard work pays off, and no one can do it for you.

Before each drill, be sure to properly warm up and hit at least five of the specific shots to be scored. When you feel ready, start scoring your performance, and then enter the results on the score sheets provided in the appendix. Use the scoring log as a diagnostic tool. Pinpoint your weaknesses and repeatedly practice those shots until your all-around level of play is acceptable to you.

Net Drill

An excellent way to develop one's play at the net, this drill consists of a scored game played entirely between the short service lines. The initial serve can be from any place on or off the court, but is most effectively made from about the intersection of the short service line and the centerline.

Advanced Clear Drill

The server and receiver should position themselves at the center base. High serves are hit randomly to positions A, B, or C (see Figure 10.1). The receiver must move from the base to the proper position for each shot and then return to the base. To make the drill worth more for conditioning, allow less time between shots. For scoring, use the target shown in Figure 9.3. After ten strokes, grade yourself: 40 +, excellent; 30–39, good; and 20–29, acceptable.

Advanced Drop Shot Drill

In this drill, ten high serves are hit rapidly, one deep, the next to center court, the next deep, and so on, requiring continuous, rapid movement of the receiver, who starts from the center base position each time. Use tape or chalk to outline a five-foot-wide target in the area between the net and the short service line, one at each side. Scoring will be: 10 on target, outstanding; 8, excellent; and 6, acceptable. (See Figure 10.1.)

Conditioning Smash Drill

The server, with a supply of at least ten shuttles, stands at center court and hits high serves to the receiver, who starts at center position, executes a smash, and returns to base after each serve. The server times the serves so that the receiver is constantly on the run, barely having time to return to center position prior to the next serve.

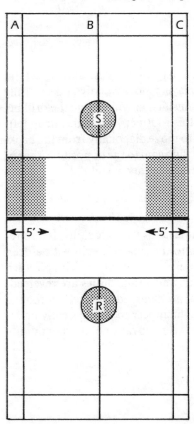

Figure 10.1 Target areas for the advanced drop shot drill.

Conditioning Clear Drill

The initial serve is high to the receiver waiting near the back line. The return is either a clear or a drop shot. The server must move up or back as necessary, hitting all clears, while the receiver stands in one spot and randomly hits clears and drop shots to the right and left. The server must return to the center position after each shot, play ending only on a missed shot. Skill and fitness will dictate the length of rallies. The two players should change duties after a predetermined number of shots, a set number of rallies, or a given period of time.

Drive Drill

This simple, yet demanding drill starts with a drive serve. Each player continues hitting drives until a mishit occurs. Aggressive play is critical because you cannot allow the shuttle to drop too low. If it does, the return will be lifted and your opponent can smash the resulting clear. Each player should try to change direction, mixing shots—down the line and crosscourt, midcourt and backcourt. Agility, quick reflexes, and skilled strokes are absolutely necessary for long rallies, which provide conditioning.

Clear and Drop Drill

The complex clear and drop drill demands fitness, mastery of strokes, and successful completion of the separate clear drill and drop drill. Both players move rapidly and skillfully through a choreographed pattern of shots until one player mishits, at which time the drill begins again. After an initial deep, high serve, each follows this routine: clear right, drop left, clear left, drop right, and so on. This requires each receiver to move diagonally from the back- to the frontcourt, then to the other back corner, and diagonally again to the opposite corner of the frontcourt. This is a great way to develop skill and fitness simultaneously!

Smash and Clear Drill

This drill requires a good feel for both the smash and the clear as separate skills. It also requires the exercise of extreme quickness in skilled reaction to the smash. Begin with a deep high serve that is smashed by the receiver. The smash is returned by clear, which is in turn smashed. This continues until one player makes an error, at which time duties are reversed. All clears must be well hit (deep); otherwise, short clears that are smashed are likely to end the rally immediately. Without a lot of movement, this drill might appear to be physically undemanding. However, if the players are both skilled enough to keep the rally going for a minute or two, you will be surprised at how tough the smash and clear drill can be!

11
Warm-Up and Cool-Down

Warm-Up

Prior to play or practice, you should prepare the muscles of your body for the vigorous exercise ahead. Specifically, this means performing a series of light exercises to loosen your muscles and increase your circulation. This period of light exercise allows your body to gradually move from a state of inactivity to one of readiness for more vigorous and strenuous movement.

The amount of time and the type of exercises an individual employs to warm up will vary. Generally, the warm-up period lasts ten to fifteen minutes. To allow for this pregame and prepractice warm-up period, arrive in plenty of time to perform it. Start with some stretching exercises, followed by a brisk walk, then a short, thirty- to sixty-second jog, and concluding with hitting practice of shots you will eventually use in the game. Start slowly and gradually increase the tempo of the warm-up. However, do not make your warm-up the workout. The idea is to prepare your body for the contest, not to fatigue it.

Reasons for Warm-Up
- To increase blood flow
- To increase muscle and joint flexibility
- To prepare for quicker and more forceful muscle contractions (means added power)
- To reduce the number and severity of injuries
- To prevent or reduce muscle soreness
- To prepare the heart for vigorous and strenuous activity
- To enhance performance

Cool-Down

The body needs to cool down after play just as it needs to warm up prior to engaging in sports activity. This cooling-down period after play allows your body to gradually relax and readjust to a normal circulatory pattern. Stopping play abruptly tends to result in the pooling of blood in the extremities. This can cause muscle spasms or cramps as well as abnormalities in the electric pattern of the heartbeat in many people.

The cool-down period should take at least five to ten minutes. Once you finish play, walk for a short period of time. Follow this with a short period of light stretching. Do not just sit down following strenuous play. Cool down first, or you might find yourself getting dizzy because the return of blood to the heart is reduced. Avoid very cold or very hot showers right after you exercise. While icy water will reduce the heat load that results from exercise, it can also cause abrupt increases in blood pressure. On the other hand, hot showers or saunas tend to aggravate the pooling of blood away from the heart. The result can be a drop in blood pressure, dizziness, and fainting.

Exercises for Warm-Up and Cool-Down

The following stretching exercises can be used both to prepare your body for strenuous activity and to progressively cool it down after play:

- The Calf and Achilles Stretch (Figure 11.1)
- The Hamstring Stretch (Figure 11.2)
- The Toe Pointer (stretches thigh muscles) (Figure 11.3)
- The Inner Thigh Stretch (Figure 11.4)
- The Lower Back Stretch (Figure 11.5)
- The Shoulder Stretch (Figure 11.6)

Figure 11.1 The calf and achilles stretch.

Figure 11.2 The hamstring stretch.

Figure 11.3 The toe pointer.

Figure 11.4 The inner thigh stretch.

Figure 11.5 The lower back stretch.

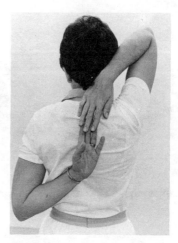

Figure 11.6 The shoulder stretch.

12
Fitness for Badminton

Why is physical fitness important for badminton? Generally, good conditioning is desirable for recreational play and an absolute necessity for tournament competition. Yet how-to-play texts often give this aspect of the sport little or no attention in spite of the fact that being physically fit not only permits one to perform closer to one's potential, it also decreases the incidence of injuries.

Playing into Shape

Some people claim that the best way to get into shape for a given sport is simply to spend time playing that sport. Clearly, an element of truth exists in this idea. Beginners, however, rarely achieve the high-intensity, action-packed play necessary to improve fitness significantly. Skilled players, if evenly matched, can push themselves hard enough in singles play to acquire a good state of fitness. Besides the fact that absolute fitness is seldom achieved by this approach, playing to fatigue often leads to sloppy mental habits and a deterioration in skill. Attempting to maintain or improve skill is extremely difficult when you are very tired. The best learning takes place under conditions of mental and physical freshness. In short, as Thomas Cureton, one of the pioneer exercise specialists, said, "You generally should not play games to get fit, but rather should get fit to play games." Prior to playing any sport, analyze the activity to design more appropriate workouts. Any exercise, given sufficient intensity or duration, will provide some fitness benefits. However, to minimize wasted motion and to maximize efficiency, the training stresses you use should be closely related to the demands of the particular sport.

Characteristics of Badminton

Badminton is an explosive game played in a discontinuous manner. It is extremely demanding in terms of agility, quickness, and power. Anaerobic power dominates. The term *anaerobic* refers to muscular activity of a short duration that requires little or no oxygen during contractions, so that the energy level is replenished between the periods of activity. This accounts for the high heart, respiratory, and oxygen delivery rates that occur during recovery periods between repeated rallying in badminton, lifting in weight training, or performing of any short-duration, high-intensity exercise. Taking this concept one step further, to more effectively deliver the oxygen to the muscles during the recovery intervals between rallies, apparently some degree of *aerobic* fitness is called for. Recognition of this fact has often led to emphasis of jogging as a basic element in getting fit for many sports. Jogging does increase the ability of your body to deliver and use larger amounts of oxygen (i.e. your *aerobic capacity*). However, it is a training mode that mimics or is more closely related to the activity pattern in distance running and is far more appropriate for marathoners than for badminton players. Aerobic fitness can also be developed by higher intensity exercise done repeatedly for relatively short periods. The key is to develop anaerobic and aerobic fitness simultaneously in a pattern specific to the demands of badminton. A person with basic badminton skills who has trained only by jogging will have difficulty retrieving shots hit deep, short, right, and left, that require a quick and explosive response. Even the most aerobically fit jogger may be humbled by intense badminton strategy. In summary, if you feel that you really need to run, short sprints at maximum to near maximum speed, separated by quick stops and intervals of walking, are the best running exercises for badminton players. This type of running more closely simulates the sudden bursts of speed that occur during play. Distance running is less efficient but does help to improve stamina.

What about strength? If power is a factor, should you spend time in the weight room? A qualified yes is the answer. The lightweight shuttlecocks and racquets are more responsive to coordinated skill than to brute strength, but the strength and ability to repeatedly get into good position allow you to make maximum use of your skilled strokes and can often compensate for lack of size and muscularity. Those players who have developed excellent form and skill but lack the power to clear or smash adequately would profit from time spent in strength development. Good strength improves speed, agility, and power. Primary attention should be given to improving leg strength because the greatest demands in badminton are on the legs. Interestingly, the next most stressed area of the body in terms of strength is the trunk. The arms need less attention because of the very light weight of the racquet and shuttle. Strength work assists in development of the anaerobic power so necessary for explosive movement. It also promotes muscular endurance for any given task (e.g., footwork in court coverage).

Weight Control

Another aspect of fitness that relates to endurance and strength is relative body fatness. Fat is detrimental to endurance, agility, and quickness. Outstanding badminton players are characterized by the lean look. We have already discussed why fitness is necessary for injury-free, top-notch badminton play: The best players are lean, quick, and agile, exhibit outstanding endurance and power, and possess at least good strength. The next step is to work toward achieving this ideal. Given enough time, excess fatness will usually take care of itself. The demands of regular, vigorous exercise of any kind serve to reduce the percentage of body fat in two ways: (1) the caloric cost of training includes the use of fat as fuel and (2) at least a small amount of added muscle tissue results, particularly from high intensity activities. While the penalty you pay for excess fatness is severe, never look for a quick and easy way out. Regular exercise over a long period of time along with minor attention to food intake will usually control weight. No real diet, as the term is generally used, is necessary. A nutritionally sound, well-balanced diet is called for. The only alterations necessary in terms of food *type* would be to change the carbohydrate-fat balance toward less fat. Few people today need to be concerned about protein—our intake of this foodstuff is generally more than adequate. The same is usually true for vitamins and minerals, unless you eat unbalanced meals. The only exception might be iron. Many women involved in sports need iron supplements.

Outside of supplements, you must consider total caloric demands, which are certainly increased with heavy exercise. The caloric cost of any activity is a function of body size. Exercise burns more calories for an overweight person than for a lean one! Table 12.1 illustrates some examples of energy consumption, all approximations that vary greatly depending on your skill level. Notice the advantage of the continuous activity, jogging, even though its intensity is less.

Table 12.1 Approximate Energy Costs of Badminton and Jogging (Kcal per minute)

	100-Pound Person	150-Pound Person	200-Pound Person
Badminton			
Novice	3.5	5.2	7.0
One course	5.0	7.5	10.0
Expert	6.5	9.7	13.0
Jogging			
10-min mile	9.0	13.0	18.0
8-min mile	11.0	16.0	22.0
6-min mile	14.0	21.0	28.0

When beginning training, let your appetite dictate caloric intake. The increase in calories used in exercise is usually *not* matched by a naturally occurring increase in appetite. In fact, sometimes a lag in appetite results in weight loss. However, if one is obese and no weight change occurs after one or two months, some *slight* curtailment of caloric intake is necessary. Remember—avoid crash diets and quick weight losses! These are unhealthy at best; to a person engaged in heavy physical activity, they impose a severe additional physical stress. For players of close to normal weight, exercise often results in a little added muscle and a little lost fat—no weight change, but a vastly more healthy condition!

Quickness and Agility

Quickness is largely predetermined by genetic factors. A dominance of fast-twitch muscle fibers is best for badminton players, while slow-twitch skeletal muscle fibers serve the marathoner well. The ability to anticipate your opponent's moves and strikes is often mistaken for quickness. This is not a physiologic characteristic, but rather comes with experience and study of the game. Apparently, we can do little to modify our physiologic quickness, but analysis and lots of practice can partially compensate for any such disadvantage. Agility, on the other hand, is negatively affected by excess body mass, particularly fat. It can be improved by increasing your leg strength and developing proper footwork habits.

Applying Fitness Principles

The idea that you will gain in fitness in proportion to your investment of time and effort is a myth. You can reach a point of diminishing returns or a point where deterioration in performance occurs (overtraining or staleness). Exercise is a stress, and the body's ability to handle stress is limited. Exercise stress superimposed on illness, fatigue, too-little sleep, undernutrition, or environmental extremes such as high altitude can result in problems. These problems can be minor, such as a limited ability to train hard, or they can result in serious injury or even death. The need to improve your condition for competition should be tempered with common sense. Ease up or skip workouts whenever potential difficulties arise.

Change of Pace in Training

Another misconception about training is that you need to always maintain about the same level of exercise, or you will lose fitness and performance. The fact of the matter is that vastly different workouts should be planned for about a month preceding and during a competitive season. For an introductory, one-semester badminton class, you should strive early for large volumes of low-intensity work that will build an endurance base. As you get well into the season or class, the volume of work decreases while intensity increases. More and more time is spent on skill, power, and strength rather than endurance. (See Figure 12.1.) This is true whether you jog, train with weights, or engage in specific badminton drills. When tournament play begins, almost all practice time should be spent in high-quality work on drills involving skills and strategy. Optimal conditioning should have been achieved, and little or no off-the-court work is necessary for maintenance. To take part in much pure conditioning work after the heavy competitive season begins is a serious mistake. The volume of such work, if any, should be very low, with the emphasis on high intensity. Strive for quality, and keep quantity at a minimum.

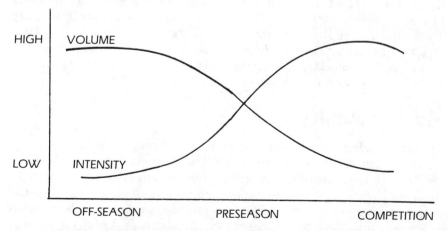

Figure 12.1 Periodization of Volume and Intensity in physical conditioning, moving from high-volume, low-intensity in the off-season to high-intensity, low-volume for competition.

Realistic Goal Setting

When planning in-season workouts, keep in mind that you should always consider (1) where you are (present fitness and skill) and (2) where you want to be (goals). You can play at an infinite number of levels in badminton, ranging from those that require little or no fitness to the all-consuming international-class play engaged in by superbly conditioned athletes. As a rule of thumb in deciding the proper level of training for your particular set of circumstances, ask yourself these questions:

1. Am I excessively fatigued after a practice or workout session?
2. Do I approach the next day's practice or workout already tired or with dread?

If the answer to either question is yes, then reexamine your practice habits. A fine line exists between the amount of physical stress needed for optimal conditioning and the level that will bring on the physical deterioration and loss of motivation of overtraining. Individual attention to cumulative fatigue and motivation along with an understanding of the science of conditioning will allow you to properly monitor your personal training needs.

All Work and No Play

After a period of concentrated work, whether a competitive season or a semester of badminton, a change of pace is recommended. One should maintain an active, recreative life-style that will allow the body and mind a chance to recuperate. Alternative games, hiking, canoeing, or other such activities will prevent a severe drop-off in fitness, minimizing the task of reestablishing playing condition. The whole idea behind this variable approach to training is to achieve maximum efficiency. By manipulating the volume and intensity of work, you can effectively carry out an off-season fitness program that will allow you to work gradually into condition and obtain peak performance at the proper time. This will help you to avoid injuries while making the most of your natural ability.

Fitness as a Lifetime Commitment

Limiting your physical conditioning to the semester in which you are involved in badminton (or another sport) is a short-sighted approach. While most people play sports and games for the relaxation and fun they afford, one should engage in a primary, regular physical activity to maintain health and fitness. Aiming for fitness on a semester- or other short-term basis is foolish. Fitness should be a lifetime commitment. The real payoff is in middle age and later, when those who have remained active from youth are as healthy as those who are decades younger. A few of the benefits of a life of continuous conditioning are: less susceptibility to cardiovascular disease; maintenance of lung function; minimal loss of strength, muscular endurance, and flexibility; easier weight control; better resistance to all sorts of stresses (whether psychological or environmental); and a positive self-concept along with other psychological benefits. Badminton and other sports are simply tools that should be kept in perspective. They are a means toward an end—the achievement of a happier, healthier life.

Supplementary Running for Optimal Fitness

Table 12.2 is an example of a running training program for a young, healthy adult. It illustrates the basic approach of moving from a low-intensity and high-volume regimen at the outset to a high-intensity and low-volume program during competitive play. While the training

Table 12.2   *Supplementary Running Program For a Young Adult*

Phase	Week	Exercise	Load	Frequency
Preparatory	1	walk/jog	3.0 miles/30 min	(M,T,Th,F,S)
(before the	2	jog	2½ miles/22½ min	(M,T,Th,F,S)
semester begins)	3	jog	2¼ miles/18 min	(M,T,Th,F)
	4	jog	2 miles/14 min	(M,W,F)
Competition	1–2	440 yds × 7	80% best time*	(3 days/wk)**
(during the	3–4	220 yds × 8	85% best time*	(3 days/wk)**
semester)	5–6	110 yds × 12	90% best time*	(2 days/wk)**
	7–8	50 yds × 18	95% best time*	(2 days/wk)**
	9–16	Replace running with high intensity conditioning/skill drills on noncompetition class days.		
Transition	1	jog 1.0 mile 6:30		(2×/wk)
	2	jog 1½ miles 10:30		(3×/wk)
	3	jog 2.0 miles 14:30		(4×/wk)
	4	jog 2.5 miles 19:30		(4×/wk)
	5+	jog 3.0 miles 24:00		(5×/wk)

*Allow enough walking recovery between repetitions to allow the heart rate to drop below 120 beats per min.
**Schedule interval work on nonclass days.

program is meant for an individual involved in a semester of badminton instruction, the *concept* holds true for high-level competitors and for other sports. Within this context, adjustments in frequencies, distances, and speeds should be made on an individual basis. (See Figure 12.2.)

Fine-Tuning Strength and Endurance

Most of the muscular strength and endurance needed for badminton can be obtained using standard calisthenic exercises as a supplement to running and playing the game itself. For those who seek optimal fitness for badminton, some attention to resistance training with weights is necessary. In any event, you should manipulate this phase of conditioning as you would any other—larger volume and lower intensity early in the training program, reversing the emphasis in order to *peak* at tournament time. Warm up well in advance of any high-intensity workout. Some examples of proper procedures are shown in Table 12.3. This is a highly idealistic approach, particularly useful to those who are extremely well motivated to succeed

Table 12.3 Example of Application of the Theory of Periodization in Supplementary Weight Training

Exercises	Preseason Preparation	Preseason Transition	In-season Competition
Squats, leg curls, pullovers, wrist curls, reverse wrist curls, bench presses	3 sets of 10 reps (low intensity)	3 sets of 5 reps (high intensity)	2 sets of 3 reps (highest intensity)

in badminton. Most people will have neither the interest nor the time for such high-level conditioning. However, an understanding of these concepts is a requisite for all who might wish at some later date to participate with great expectations for success in badminton or in another sport.

Instead of standard pull-ups, those players who do not have adequate strength to do this exercise may substitute bar hangs. (See Figure 12.3.) To perform this exercise, grasp the bar with the arms bent so that your chin is about bar height. Hold this position as long as possible, then lower yourself slowly while resisting to the best of your ability. For those who cannot do regular push-ups, rest on your hands and knees rather than on the hands and toes while doing this exercise. Sit-ups should be done with the angle of the knee at about ninety degrees and the feet stabilized by another person or an object.

Back hyperextensions require special mention. Along with sit-ups, they help to develop muscles important in preventing low back pain. Begin this exercise by aiming the head and torso downward, with a partner stabilizing the legs and hips on a high bench or table. The

Figure 12.2 Jogging is an excellent conditioner.   **Figure 12.3** Bar hang.   Pull-up.

hands are clasped behind, at the small of the back. The body and head are then raised as high as possible before returning to the starting position. (See Figure 12.4.)

Half squats or parallel squats are performed with a barbell held on the shoulders. Move to a position in which the thighs are parallel to the floor, either with the feet flat on the floor or with heels on a two-by-four-inch board if lack of flexibility is a problem. For those players unfamiliar with weight training on a regular basis, one of several kinds of squat racks that are made for safety should be used when performing this exercise. (See Figure 12.5.)

Figure 12.4 Back hyperextensions.

Figure 12.5 Half squats

Pullovers are done with the arms bent at the elbows. Lie on a bench with your head at one end, knees bent, and feet on the other end. Move the barbell from the chest over the head and as near to the floor as possible without arching your back. Pull the weight over to your chest and repeat the exercise. (See Figure 12.6.)

Dumbbells are used for the flys and the inverted flys. The former is done from a supine position on a bench. The dumbbells are moved from the arms-extended position up until they cross at the chest. Until you develop good strength, maintain some arm bend at the elbow. The inverted fly, sometimes called the lateral raise, maybe done either from a prone position on a bench or from a standing, forward-bending position with the trunk almost parallel to the floor. Either way, the dumbbells are moved under control from the low position upward as high as possible and then returned. (See Figure 12.7.)

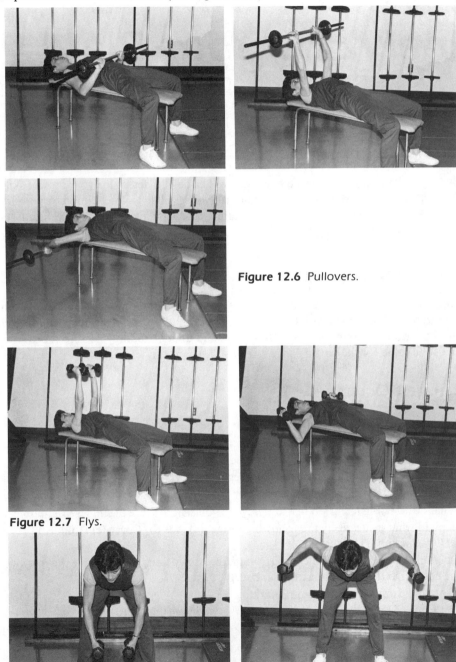

Figure 12.6 Pullovers.

Figure 12.7 Flys.

Inverted flys.

13
Analyzing Your Play

By testing yourself at regular intervals, you will be able to determine your present skill level and then plan a program of practice drills and study that will help you to improve your level of play. You can use several methods to determine your current level of badminton competence—in skill, technique, and general knowledge of the game.

Knowledge Exams

Both written and oral examinations can be taken to find out how much information and understanding of badminton you have acquired pertaining to rules, strategy, and techniques of play. The two important factors—knowledge and understanding—lead to a better appreciation of the game for the participant as well as the spectator.

Written Test Questions

1. Name the offensive shots of the game. Describe their execution and use.
2. List the defensive shots of the game. Describe their execution and use.
3. Name and describe the various serves used during play.
4. Describe the factors that constitute an illegal serve.
5. Explain what is meant by a *let*.
6. What does *setting* mean? When and how do you *set* the score in singles? In doubles?
7. Explain what is meant by the following terms: (a) Ace (b) Carry (c) Double hit (d) Fault (e) Obstruction (f) Poach
8. Diagram a badminton singles court. State the dimensions and identify the markings on the court. Do the same for a doubles court.
9. Explain the purpose of the court markings.
10. List some of the factors one should consider when selecting a racquet.
11. Ideally, how many officials are needed to officiate a match? Name and explain their duties and responsibilities.

12. What are the characteristics of an official shuttle? How is a shuttle selected for tournament play?

13. Indicate the most strategic position in singles for receiving the serve in the right-hand service court. Explain. In the left-hand service court? Explain.

14. Indicate the most strategic position in singles during a rally. Explain.

15. What is the proper position for receiving the serve in doubles when the shuttle is served to the right service court? Explain. To the left service court? Explain.

16. Name and explain the different methods of positioning that can be used during a doubles game. What is considered the best method? Explain. What is the least effective method? Explain.

17. Describe the essentials in hitting the following strokes: (a) Forehand (b) Backhand (c) Underhand (d) Overhand (e) Round-the-Head

18. What is meant by *wrist cock?* Explain both the forehand and backhand methods of cocking the wrist.

19. What is meant by *warm-up?* Why is it necessary? Describe an appropriate warm-up routine.

20. What is meant by *cool down?* Why is it necessary? Describe an appropriate cool-down routine.

21. How does conditioning affect a player's performance in badminton?

22. What agency governs badminton play in the United States? Internationally?

23. What methods can be employed to improve the following? (a) Cardiorespiratory endurance (b) Muscle strength (c) Muscle endurance (d) Flexibility and mobility

24. Explain how to select a partner for doubles.

25. What is meant by the following terms? (a) Singles (b) Doubles (c) Mixed doubles

26. Name some procedures that can be used to evaluate a player's badminton knowledge and skill. Explain.

27. Name and explain some drills that can be used to improve a player's proficiency in: (a) Stroke performance (b) Shot execution (c) Serving (d) Footwork

28. What is meant by a high percentage shot? Explain. A low percentage shot? Explain.

29. Describe how to select the following for badminton play: (a) Clothing (b) Racquet (c) Footwear

30. What are some of the benefits of regular play? Explain.

Skill Tests

Badminton proficiency can also be evaluated through the use of skill tests. These tests will provide you with tangible proof of your progress in performing a particular skill. In addition to measuring your performance, they also make excellent practice routines.

Use the skill performance activities presented in Chapter 9 to measure your performance, and record your test results in the appendix logs. In this way, you can keep a record of your progress.

Badminton Shot and Serve Evaluation and Scouting Charts

These charts provide a way to objectively collect data and analyze shot and serve performance under actual game conditions. Although *one game is not conclusive,* the factual data will provide insight concerning the strengths and weaknesses of a player's game. (See Figures 13.1 and 13.2.)

They also serve as excellent instruments for gathering pertinent data about your opponent's skill and style of play. With the information you collect and your own knowledge and understanding of badminton, you can devise an intelligent game plan. Completed charts contain data pertaining to the shots and serves employed to win rallies or commit errors during a contest. Once you have concrete facts about your own and your opponent's strengths and weaknesses, you can use this specific information to design your practice sessions and a sound plan of attack.

How to Use the Charts

1. Ask another player who has at least a basic understanding of the game to help you.
2. Instruct this person on how to record results in the appropriate boxes.
   a. Place a dot in the box opposite the name for each shot or serve that is hit for a winner or results in an error.
   b. After the game, total the number of dots in each box.
   c. When more than one game is recorded, total the numbers for each game in the appropriate boxes.
3. Examine and analyze the data after you have completed item 2 above.
4. Interpret the information and design your practice sessions and game plan accordingly.

Note: If you are scouting a future opponent, you can collect the data by yourself and follow the procedures in item two.

How to Interpret the Charts

After you have several completed shot and serve evaluation charts in your possession, the next step is to examine and analyze their contents. From these charts, you should be able to determine your own and your opponent's strengths, weaknesses, and playing tendencies. The charts will factually point out the shots and serves relied on most often to score points, force errors, or cause weak returns.

The Shot Evaluation Chart is divided into the five primary shots employed in badminton play. It is further subdivided to help distinguish and detect any strengths and weaknesses in the forehand, backhand, and around-the-head strokes.

The Serve Evaluation Chart indicates the four predominant serves employed during play. Subdivisions indicate court areas and service results. By breaking it down this way, you will be able to know the frequency of serves to a particular area and the end result of each serve.

DATE: _____			SMASH			DROP			DRIVE		ATTACK CLEAR		HIGH CLEAR		HAIRPIN	
GAME #																
PARTICIPANTS			BH	FH	AH	BH	FH	AH	BH	FH	BH	FH	BH	FH	BH	FH
	W															
	E															
	W															
	E															

LEGEND
BH: BACKHAND
FH: FOREHAND
AH: AROUND-THE-HEAD

W: WINNING SHOT
E: MISSED SHOT/ERROR/WEAK RETURN

Figure 13.1 Badminton shot evaluation and scouting chart.

DATE:

GAME #

PARTICIPANTS	SERVE RESULT	LOW SERVE				HIGH SERVE				DRIVE SERVE				FLICK SERVE			
		LEFT		RIGHT		LEFT		RIGHT		LEFT		RIGHT		LEFT		RIGHT	
		LC	RC	LC	RC	LC	RC	LC	RC	LC	RC	LC	RC	LC	RC	LC	RC
	ACE																
	ERROR																
	POOR																
	GOOD																
	ACE																
	ERROR																
	POOR																
	GOOD																

LEFT: Left receiving court
RIGHT: Right receiving court
LC: Left corner of receiving court
RC: Right corner of receiving court

ACE: Outright winning serve
ERROR: Miss or serve does not land in receiving court
POOR: A serve that is easy to return (one that is returned with an offensive shot)
GOOD: A serve that is difficult to return (one that must be returned with a defensive shot)

Figure 13.2 Badminton serve evaluation and scouting chart.

These two charts are very simple to prepare and use. As you learn more about the game, you can devise a chart that is more complex. How detailed you design it will depend upon the data you wish to obtain. Several Shot and Serve Evaluation and Scouting Charts are located in Appendix J for your use.

The Tournament Test

The ultimate test of a player's ability is measured in the win-loss column in league or tournament play. Regardless of how well you score on a knowledge or skills test, the true measure of your progress and ability is your cumulative record in competition.

Many different types of tournament play are offered in physical education classes, intramural-recreational sports programs, city recreational competition, and sanctioned badminton championships. They include single-elimination, double-elimination, consolation, round-robin, and challenge tournaments. The most reliable of these to evaluate a player's ability in relation to a particular group is the *round-robin tournament*. The results of this type of tournament provide the most valid appraisal of an individual's performance because each player has to play every other player.

Single-, double-, or *consolation-elimination tournaments* afford the opportunity for players to gain competitive experience but are unsatisfactory as evaluation instruments. A player may win or lose without playing against every other player. Even the most skilled player can have an "off" day or be eliminated early in the competition.

Challenge tournaments allow for lots of play. They are conducted over a long period of time and are another way of ranking performance. The most frequently used of the challenge tournaments is the *ladder*. To start, each player is listed or ranked numerically through the use of various methods—alphabetically, early sign-up, lottery, previous tournament performance, etc. The participants are allowed to challenge players ranked one or two rungs above them on the ladder in an attempt to reach the highest rung. The winner is the player whose name is listed on the top rung of the ladder when the period of competition has ended. The rules for such a tournament are generally determined by the number of players participating, the amount of facilities, and the time available.

Summary

As you can see, many different methods can be used to assist you in measuring your progress. Each of them provides you with pertinent data. Collectively, they give you an excellent indication of your ability and understanding of the game. Also, some of these instruments can be employed to ascertain factual data about your opponent. Once you have this data, it will be up to you to put it to good use.

Appendix A: Badminton Match Log

Recording Instructions

1. Write the name of your opponent (singles) or opponents (doubles) in the first column.
2. Record the scores for each game in the next three columns.
3. Total the score for all the games, and record them in the column marked *Total Points*.
4. Record the date, time, and place of the match.
5. Make comments where appropriate.

NAME: _____

OPPONENT(S)	GAME 1		GAME 2		GAME 3		TOTAL POINTS		DATE / TIME	PLACE	COMMENTS
	YOU	OPP.	YOU	OPP.	YOU	OPP.	YOU	OPP.			

GAME RECORD: WINS _____ LOSSES _____
MATCH RECORD: WINS _____ LOSSES _____

Appendix B: Badminton Short Serve Skill Test Log

Recording Instructions

1. Allow five practice serves.
2. Record in the boxes marked *Target Score* the actual score per trial (where the shuttle strikes the target zone).
3. Record in the boxes marked *Bonus Score* 1 point per trial if the shuttle travels over the net and below a rope divider that is placed twenty inches above and parallel to the net. For serves traveling above the rope or hit into the net, a score of 0 is placed in the bonus box.
4. Total and average the score after all ten trials are completed.
5. Make comments where appropriate.

NAME: _____ DATE: _____ TIME: _____ PLACE: _____

TEST NO: _____ RECORDER: _____

	TRIALS										TOTAL SCORE	AVG. SCORE	COMMENTS
	1	2	3	4	5	6	7	8	9	10			
BONUS SCORE PER TRIAL													
TARGET SCORE PER TRIAL													
TOTAL SCORE PER TRIAL													

NAME: _____ DATE: _____ TIME: _____ PLACE: _____

TEST NO: _____ RECORDER: _____

	TRIALS										TOTAL SCORE	AVG. SCORE	COMMENTS
	1	2	3	4	5	6	7	8	9	10			
BONUS SCORE PER TRIAL													
TARGET SCORE PER TRIAL													
TOTAL SCORE PER TRIAL													

NAME: _____ DATE: _____ TIME: _____ PLACE: _____

TEST NO: _____ RECORDER: _____

	TRIALS										TOTAL SCORE	AVG. SCORE	COMMENTS
	1	2	3	4	5	6	7	8	9	10			
BONUS SCORE PER TRIAL													
TARGET SCORE PER TRIAL													
TOTAL SCORE PER TRIAL													

NAME: _____ DATE: _____ TIME: _____ PLACE: _____

TEST NO: _____ RECORDER: _____

	TRIALS										TOTAL SCORE	AVG. SCORE	COMMENTS
	1	2	3	4	5	6	7	8	9	10			
BONUS SCORE PER TRIAL													
TARGET SCORE PER TRIAL													
TOTAL SCORE PER TRIAL													

NAME: _____ DATE: _____ TIME: _____ PLACE: _____

TEST NO: _____ RECORDER: _____

	TRIALS										TOTAL SCORE	AVG. SCORE	COMMENTS
	1	2	3	4	5	6	7	8	9	10			
BONUS SCORE PER TRIAL													
TARGET SCORE PER TRIAL													
TOTAL SCORE PER TRIAL													

NAME: _____ DATE: _____ TIME: _____ PLACE: _____

TEST NO: _____ RECORDER: _____

	TRIALS										TOTAL SCORE	AVG. SCORE	COMMENTS
	1	2	3	4	5	6	7	8	9	10			
BONUS SCORE PER TRIAL													
TARGET SCORE PER TRIAL													
TOTAL SCORE PER TRIAL													

NAME: _____ DATE: _____ TIME: _____ PLACE: _____

TEST NO: _____ RECORDER: _____

	TRIALS										TOTAL SCORE	AVG. SCORE	COMMENTS
	1	2	3	4	5	6	7	8	9	10			
BONUS SCORE PER TRIAL													
TARGET SCORE PER TRIAL													
TOTAL SCORE PER TRIAL													

NAME: _____ DATE: _____ TIME: _____ PLACE: _____

TEST NO: _____ RECORDER: _____

	TRIALS										TOTAL SCORE	AVG. SCORE	COMMENTS
	1	2	3	4	5	6	7	8	9	10			
BONUS SCORE PER TRIAL													
TARGET SCORE PER TRIAL													
TOTAL SCORE PER TRIAL													

NAME: _____ DATE: _____ TIME: _____ PLACE: _____

TEST NO: _____ RECORDER: _____

	TRIALS										TOTAL SCORE	AVG. SCORE	COMMENTS
	1	2	3	4	5	6	7	8	9	10			
BONUS SCORE PER TRIAL													
TARGET SCORE PER TRIAL													
TOTAL SCORE PER TRIAL													

NAME: _____ DATE: _____ TIME: _____ PLACE: _____

TEST NO: _____ RECORDER: _____

	TRIALS										TOTAL SCORE	AVG. SCORE	COMMENTS
	1	2	3	4	5	6	7	8	9	10			
BONUS SCORE PER TRIAL													
TARGET SCORE PER TRIAL													
TOTAL SCORE PER TRIAL													

NAME: _____ DATE: _____ TIME: _____ PLACE: _____

TEST NO: _____ RECORDER: _____

	TRIALS										TOTAL SCORE	AVG. SCORE	COMMENTS
	1	2	3	4	5	6	7	8	9	10			
BONUS SCORE PER TRIAL													
TARGET SCORE PER TRIAL													
TOTAL SCORE PER TRIAL													

Appendix C: Badminton Long Serve Skill Test Log

Recording Instructions

1. Allow five practice serves.
2. Record the date and time of the test in column 1.
3. Write the test number and the name of the person recording the score in the next column.
4. Record in the ten boxes under the section *Trials* the actual score for each trial (where the shuttle strikes the target zone).
5. Total and then average the score for the ten trials.
6. Make comments where appropriate.

NAME: _____

DATE / TIME	TEST NO. / RECORDER	TRIALS 1	2	3	4	5	6	7	8	9	10	TOTAL SCORE	AVG. SCORE	COMMENTS

Appendix D: Badminton Clear Shot Skill Test Log

Recording Instructions

1. Allow five practice shots.
2. Record the date and time of the test in column 1.
3. Write the test number and the name of the person recording the score in the next column.
4. Record in the ten boxes under the section *Trials* the actual score for each trial (where the shuttle strikes the target zone).
5. Total and then average the score for the ten trials.
6. Make comments where appropriate.

NAME: _____

DATE / TIME	TEST NO. / RECORDER	TRIALS										TOTAL SCORE	AVG. SCORE	COMMENTS
		1	2	3	4	5	6	7	8	9	10			

Appendix E: Badminton Smash Shot Skill Test Log

NAME: _____

DATE / TIME	TEST NO. / RECORDER	TRIALS										TOTAL SCORE	AVG. SCORE	COMMENTS
		1	2	3	4	5	6	7	8	9	10			

NOTE: Follow the instructions given in Appendix D Badminton Clear Shot Skill Test Log.

Appendix D: Badminton Clear Shot Skill Test Log

Recording Instructions

1. Allow five practice shots.
2. Record the date and time of the test in column 1.
3. Write the test number and the name of the person recording the score in the next column.
4. Record in the ten boxes under the section *Trials* the actual score for each trial (where the shuttle strikes the target zone).
5. Total and then average the score for the ten trials.
6. Make comments where appropriate.

NAME: ______________________

DATE / TIME	TEST NO. / RECORDER	TRIALS										TOTAL SCORE	AVG. SCORE	COMMENTS
		1	2	3	4	5	6	7	8	9	10			

Appendix E: Badminton Smash Shot Skill Test Log

NAME: _____

DATE / TIME	TEST NO. / RECORDER	TRIALS										TOTAL SCORE	AVG. SCORE	COMMENTS
		1	2	3	4	5	6	7	8	9	10			

NOTE: Follow the instructions given in Appendix D Badminton Clear Shot Skill Test Log.

Appendix F: Badminton Drive Shot Skill Test Log

NAME: _____

DATE / TIME	TEST NO. / RECORDER	1	2	3	4	5	6	7	8	9	10	TOTAL SCORE	AVG. SCORE	COMMENTS

NOTE: Follow the instructions given in Appendix D Badminton Clear Shot Skill Test Log.

Appendix G: Badminton Drop Shot Skill Test Log

NAME: _____

DATE / TIME	TEST NO. / RECORDER	TRIALS 1	2	3	4	5	6	7	8	9	10	TOTAL SCORE	AVG. SCORE	COMMENTS

NOTE: Follow the instructions given in Appendix D Badminton Clear Shot Skill Test Log.

Appendix H: Badminton Flick Serve Skill Test Log

NAME: _____

DATE / TIME	TEST NO. / RECORDER	TRIALS										TOTAL SCORE	AVG. SCORE	COMMENTS
		1	2	3	4	5	6	7	8	9	10			

NOTE: Follow the instructions given in Appendix D Badminton Clear Shot Skill Test Log.

Appendix I: Badminton Drive Serve Skill Test Log

NAME: _____

DATE / TIME	TEST NO. / RECORDER	TRIALS										TOTAL SCORE	AVG. SCORE	COMMENTS
		1	2	3	4	5	6	7	8	9	10			

NOTE: Follow the instructions given in Appendix D Badminton Clear Shot Skill Test Log.

Appendix J: Shot and Serve Evaluation and Scouting Charts

DATE: GAME # PARTICIPANTS		SMASH			DROP			DRIVE		ATTACK CLEAR		HIGH CLEAR		HAIRPIN	
		BH	FH	AH	BH	FH	AH	BH	FH	BH	FH	BH	FH	BH	FH
	W														
	E														
	W														
	E														

DATE: GAME # PARTICIPANTS		SMASH			DROP			DRIVE		ATTACK CLEAR		HIGH CLEAR		HAIRPIN	
		BH	FH	AH	BH	FH	AH	BH	FH	BH	FH	BH	FH	BH	FH
	W														
	E														
	W														
	E														

DATE: GAME # PARTICIPANTS		SMASH			DROP			DRIVE		ATTACK CLEAR		HIGH CLEAR		HAIRPIN	
		BH	FH	AH	BH	FH	AH	BH	FH	BH	FH	BH	FH	BH	FH
	W														
	E														
	W														
	E														

LEGEND
BH: BACKHAND
FH: FOREHAND
AH: AROUND-THE-HEAD

W: WINNING SHOT
E: MISSED SHOT/ERROR/WEAK RETURN

DATE: _____

GAME #

PARTICIPANTS	SERVE RESULT	LOW SERVE				HIGH SERVE				DRIVE SERVE				FLICK SERVE			
		LEFT		RIGHT		LEFT		RIGHT		LEFT		RIGHT		LEFT		RIGHT	
		LC	RC	LC	RC	LC	RC	LC	RC	LC	RC	LC	RC	LC	RC	LC	RC
	ACE																
	ERROR																
	POOR																
	GOOD																
	ACE																
	ERROR																
	POOR																
	GOOD																

DATE: _____

GAME #

PARTICIPANTS	SERVE RESULT	LOW SERVE				HIGH SERVE				DRIVE SERVE				FLICK SERVE			
		LEFT		RIGHT		LEFT		RIGHT		LEFT		RIGHT		LEFT		RIGHT	
		LC	RC	LC	RC	LC	RC	LC	RC	LC	RC	LC	RC	LC	RC	LC	RC
	ACE																
	ERROR																
	POOR																
	GOOD																
	ACE																
	ERROR																
	POOR																
	GOOD																

LEFT: Left receiving court
RIGHT: Right receiving court
LC: Left corner of receiving court
RC: Right corner of receiving court

ACE: Outright winning serve
ERROR: Miss or serve does not land in receiving court
POOR: A serve that is easy to return (one that is returned with an offensive shot)
GOOD: A serve that is difficult to return (one that must be returned with a defensive shot)

120